UNDERSTANDING AND USING

English Grammar

FIFTH EDITION
WORKBOOK
VOLUME A

Betty S. Azar
Stacy A. Hagen
Geneva Tesh
Rachel Spack Koch

Understanding and Using English Grammar, Fifth Edition
Workbook, Volume A

Pearson Education, 221 River Street, Hoboken, NJ 07030

Azar Associates: Sue Van Etten, Manager

Staff credits: The people who made up the *Understanding and Using
English Grammar Fifth Edition, Workbook* team, representing content creation,
design, manufacturing, project management, publishing, rights management, and
testing, are Pietro Alongi, Rhea Banker, Stephanie Bullard, Warren Fischbach,
Nancy Flaggman, Gosia Jaros-White, Amy McCormick, Brian Panker,
Lindsay Richman, Robert Ruvo, Paula Van Ells, and Joseph Vella.

Contributing Editors: Jennifer McAliney, Janice Baillie

Text composition: Aptara

Illustrations: Don Martinetti–pages 113, 131; Chris Pavely–pages 4, 5, 46, 52, 66, 71, 89

Photo Credits—page 1: Nataliia Pyzhova/Fotolia; 13: Olly/Fotolia; 24: Samott/Fotolia; 35: Syda
    Productions/Fotolia; 43: JStone/Shutterstock; 50: RTimages/Fotolia; 63: Markop/Fotolia; 69: Blackday/
    Fotolia; 75: Sean Pavone/123RF; 83: Goku/Fotolia; 96: Chee Onn Leong/Fotolia; 107 (left): Enrico
    Della Pietra/Fotolia; 107 (right): Thomas Cockrem/Alamy Stock Photo.

ISBN 10: 0-13-427625-6
ISBN 13: 978-0-13-427625-0

Printed in the United States of America
8 2023

Contents

Preface to the Fifth Edition vi

The titles listed below refer to section names, not practice titles. In general, one section has multiple exercises. The chart numbers refer to the grammar explanations in the *Understanding and Using English Grammar* Student Book.

Chapter 1   PRESENT AND PAST; SIMPLE AND PROGRESSIVE 1
     1-1   Simple Present and Present Progressive 1
     1-2   Simple Present and Present Progressive: Affirmative, Negative,
           Question Forms 2
     1-3   Verbs Not Usually Used in the Progressive (Stative Verbs) 3
     1-4   Simple Past Tense 4
     1-5   Simple Past vs. Past Progressive 7
     1-6   Unfulfilled Intentions: *Was/Were Going To* 9

Chapter 2   PERFECT AND PERFECT PROGRESSIVE TENSES 13
     2-1   Regular and Irregular Verbs 14
     2-2   Irregular Verb List 14
     2-3   Present Perfect: *Since* and *For* 14
     2-4   Present Perfect: Unspecified Time and Repeated Events 14
     2-5   *Have* and *Has* in Spoken English 17
     2-6   Present Perfect vs. Simple Past 18
     2-7   Present Perfect Progressive 19
     2-8   Past Perfect 20
     2-10   Past Perfect Progressive 22

Chapter 3   FUTURE TIME 24
     3-1   Simple Future: Forms of *Will* and *Be Going To* 24
     3-2   *Will* vs. *Be Going To* 26
     3-3   Expressing the Future in Time Clauses 28
     3-4   Using the Present Progressive and the Simple Present to Express
           Future Time 29
     3-5   Future Progressive 31
     3-6   Future Perfect and Future Perfect Progressive 32

Chapter 4   REVIEW OF VERB TENSES 35

Chapter 5   SUBJECT-VERB AGREEMENT 43
     5-1   Final *-s/-es:* Use and Spelling 43
     5-2   Basic Subject-Verb Agreement 44
     5-3   Collective Nouns 44
     5-4   Subject-Verb Agreement: Using Expressions of Quantity 45

| | 5-5 | Subject-Verb Agreement: Using *There + Be* | 45 |
| | 5-6 | Subject-Verb Agreement: Some Irregularities | 46 |

Chapter 6   NOUNS **50**

	6-1	Regular and Irregular Plural Nouns	50
	6-2	Nouns as Adjectives	51
	6-3	Possessive Nouns	53
	6-4	More About Expressing Possession	55
	6-5	Count and Noncount Nouns	56
	6-6	Noncount Nouns	56
	6-7	Some Common Noncount Nouns	56
	6-8	Expressions of Quantity Used with Count and Noncount Nouns	57
	6-9	Using *A Few* and *Few; A Little* and *Little*	58
	6-10	Singular Expressions of Quantity: *One, Each, Every*	60
	6-11	Using *Of* in Expressions of Quantity	61

Chapter 7   ARTICLES **63**

	7-1	Articles (*A, An, The*) with Indefinite and Definite Nouns	63
	7-2	Articles: Generic Nouns	65
	7-3	Descriptive Information with Definite and Indefinite Nouns	65
	7-4	General Guidelines for Article Usage	66
	7-5	Using *The* or Ø with Titles and Geographic Names	67

Chapter 8   PRONOUNS **69**

	8-1	Pronouns and Possessive Adjectives	69
	8-2	Agreement with Generic Nouns and Indefinite Pronouns	70
	8-3	Personal Pronouns: Agreement with Collective Nouns	71
	8-4	Reflexive Pronouns	71
	8-5	Using *You, One*, and *They* as Impersonal Pronouns	72
	8-6	Forms of *Other*	72
	8-7	Common Expressions with *Other*	74

Chapter 9   MODALS, PART 1 .... **75**

	9-1	Basic Modal Introduction	75
	9-2	Expressing Necessity: *Must, Have To, Have Got To*	75
	9-3	Lack of Necessity (*Not Have To*) and Prohibition (*Must Not*)	75
	9-4	Advisability/Suggestions: *Should, Ought To, Had Better, Could*	77
	9-5	Expectation: *Be Supposed To/Should*	79
	9-6	Ability: *Can, Know How To*, and *Be Able To*	79
	9-7	Possibility: *Can, May, Might*	80
	9-8	Requests and Responses with Modals	80
	9-9	Polite Requests with *Would You Mind*	81
	9-10	Making Suggestions: *Let's, Why Don't, Shall I/We*	82

Chapter 10   MODALS, PART 2 .... **83**

	10-1	Using *Would* to Express a Repeated Action in the Past	83
	10-2	Expressing the Past: Necessity, Advice, Expectation	84
	10-3	Expressing Past Ability	86
	10-4	Degrees of Certainty: Present Time	86
	10-5	Degrees of Certainty: Present Time Negative	88
	10-6	Degrees of Certainty: Past Time	88
	10-7	Degrees of Certainty: Future Time	91
	10-8	Progressive Forms of Modals	92
	10-9	Combining Modals with Phrasal Modals	92
	10-10	Expressing Preference: *Would Rather*	93

Chapter 11   THE PASSIVE 96
           11-1   Active vs. Passive 96
           11-2   Tense Forms of the Passive 96
           11-3   Using the Passive 100
           11-4   The Passive Form of Modals and Phrasal Modals 102
           11-5   Stative (Non-Progressive) Passive 103
           11-6   Common Stative (Non-Progressive) Passive Verbs + Prepositions 103
           11-7   The Passive with *Get* 104
           11-8   *-ed/-ing* Adjectives 105

Appendix   SUPPLEMENTARY GRAMMAR CHARTS 109
   Unit A: Basic Grammar Terminology 109
           A-1   Subjects, Verbs, and Objects 109
           A-2   Adjectives 109
           A-3   Adverbs 109
           A-4   Prepositions and Prepositional Phrases 111
           A-5   Preposition Combinations with Adjectives and Adverbs 111

   Unit B: Questions 114
           B-1   Forms of Yes/No and Information Questions 114
           B-2   Question Words 115
           B-3   Shortened Yes/No Questions 118
           B-4   Negative Questions 118
           B-5   Tag Questions 119

   Unit C: Contractions 119

   Unit D: Negatives 120
           D-1   Using *Not* and Other Negative Words 120
           D-2   Avoiding Double Negatives 120
           D-3   Beginning a Sentence with a Negative Word 120

   Unit E: Verbs 121
           E-2   Spelling of *-ing* and *-ed* Verb Forms 121
           E-3   Overview of Verb Tenses 122
           E-4   Summary of Verb Tenses 123
           E-7   Linking Verbs 124
           E-8   *Raise/Rise, Set/Sit, Lay/Lie* 125

Special Workbook Section   PHRASAL VERBS 127

INDEX 137

ANSWER KEY 140

Preface

The *Understanding and Using English Grammar Workbook* is a self-study textbook. It is keyed to the explanatory grammar charts found in *Understanding and Using English Grammar, Fifth Edition,* a classroom teaching text for English language learners, as well as in the accompanying *Chartbook,* a reference grammar with no exercises. Students can use the *Workbook* independently to enhance their understanding of English structures. Students can choose from a variety of exercises that will help them use English meaningfully and correctly.

This *Workbook* is also a resource for teachers who need exercise material for additional classwork, homework, testing, or individualized instruction.

The answers to the practices can be found in the *Answer Key* in the back of the *Workbook.* Its pages are perforated so that they can be detached to make a separate booklet. However, if teachers want to use the *Workbook* as a classroom teaching text, the *Answer Key* can be removed at the beginning of the term.

A special *Workbook* section called *Phrasal Verbs,* not available in the main text, is included in the *Appendix.* This section provides a reference list of common phrasal verbs along with a variety of exercises for independent practice.

CHAPTER 1

Present and Past; Simple and Progressive

PRACTICE 1 ▶ Preview.
Read the passage. <u>Underline</u> the 11 verbs.

Indoor Plants

Many people <u>keep</u> indoor house plants for their natural beauty, but these plants also create a healthier living space. While scientists at NASA (National Aeronautics and Space Administration) were researching air quality in space stations, they discovered that common indoor house plants actually clean the air. The plants absorb carbon dioxide and release oxygen. NASA scientists found that plants also eliminate harmful chemicals in the air. In 1989, NASA published the first results of the NASA Clean Air Study. Today, scientists are still learning about the many benefits of houseplants.

---

1. Write the six verbs in the simple present tense.

   _____*keep,*_____

2. Write the three verbs in the simple past tense.

   _____

3. Write the verb in the present progressive tense.

   _____

4. Write the verb in the past progressive tense.

   _____

PRACTICE 2 ▶ The simple present and the present progressive. (Chart 1-1)
Complete the sentences. Write the simple present or the present progressive form of the verbs in parentheses.

1. a. The sun (*set*) _____*sets*_____ in the west every evening.

   b. Look! The sun (*set*) _____*is setting*_____ behind the mountain now. How beautiful!

2. a. Bring an umbrella. It (*rain*) _____.

   b. It (*rain*) _____ a lot in the spring.

3. a. I (*listen*) _____ to the weather report every morning.

   b. I (*listen*) _____ to the weather report right now.

4. a. Hurricanes usually (*form*) _____ in tropical areas.

   b. A hurricane (*form*) _____ today off the coast of Florida.

5. a. Snow (*melt*) _____ as the temperature rises.

   b. The kids want to build a snowman. They need to hurry. The snow

     (*melt*) _____ .

PRACTICE 3 ▸ The simple present and the present progressive. (Chart 1-1)
Choose the correct completions.

1. a. Because of the force of gravity, objects (fall)/ are falling   down and not up.

   b. It's autumn! The leaves   fall / are falling,   and winter will soon be here.

2. a. Coffee   grows / is growing   in mountainous areas, not in deserts.

   b. Oh, you   grow / are growing   so fast, Johnny! Soon you'll be taller than your dad.

3. a. Near the Arctic Circle, the sun   shines / is shining   for more than 20 hours a day at the beginning of the summer.

   b. It's a beautiful day! The sun   shines / is shining   and the birds   sing / are singing.

4. a. A human heart   beats / is beating   about 100,000 times a day.

   b. This movie is scary! My heart   beats / is beating   rapidly.

5. a. Most people   sleep / are sleeping   seven to eight hours a night.

   b. It's already noon! Scott   sleep / is sleeping   very late today.

PRACTICE 4 ▸ The simple present and present progressive: affirmative, negative, question forms. (Chart 1-2)
Complete the questions with **Do, Does, Is, or Are**.

1. ____*Does*____ the sun rise early?

2. ____*Is*____ the earth revolving around the sun right now?

3. _____ bears live in caves?

4. _____ it raining today?

5. _____ water freeze at 32 degrees Fahrenheit (0 degrees Celsius)?

6. _____ bees make honey nearby?

7. _____ bees making honey nearby?

PRACTICE 5 ▸ The simple present and present progressive: affirmative, negative, question forms. (Chart 1-2)
Write a correct affirmative or negative statement from the questions in Practice 4.

1. The sun _____*doesn't rise*_____ in the evening.

2. The earth _____*is revolving*_____ around the sun right now.

3. Bears _____ in caves.

4. It _____ today.

5. Water _____ at 32 degrees Fahrenheit.

6. Bees _____ honey nearby.

7. Bees _____ honey nearby.

PRACTICE 6 ▸ Non-progressive verbs. (Chart 1-3)
Choose the correct completions.

1. There you are! Behind the tree. I _____ you.
   a. see   b. am seeing
   (a. see is circled)

2. My mother's hearing has been getting worse for several months. She _____ a specialist right now.
   a. see   b. is seeing

3. Do you see that man? I _____ him. He was my high school English teacher.
   a. recognize   b. am recognizing

4. My favorite actor _____ at the Paramount Theater.
   a. currently appears   b. is currently appearing

5. A: Is my voice loud enough?
   B: Yes, I _____ you.
   a. hear   b. am hearing

6. A: Aren't you having any coffee?
   B: No, I _____ tea.
   a. prefer   b. 'm preferring

7. A: What's on your mind?
   B: I _____ about my family.
   a. think   b. am thinking

8. A: Did you make a decision yet?
   B: No, I _____ your opinion.
   a. need   b. 'm needing

9. A: Why are you staring at me?
   B: You _____ your mom so much.
   a. resemble   b. are resembling

10. A: There's Dr. Jones on a motorcycle! Do you believe it?
    B: Yeah, he _____ several.
    a. owns   b. is owning

PRACTICE 7 ▸ The present progressive to describe a temporary state.
(Chart 1-3, footnote)
Choose the correct completions. If a situation describes a temporary state, choose the present progressive.

1. My husband and I are short, but our children _____.
   a. are tall   b. are being tall
   (a. are tall is circled)

2. Jane's an intelligent woman, but she won't see a doctor about those headaches she has.

   She _____.
   a. is foolish   b. is being foolish

3. The teacher spoke harshly to the children because they were too noisy, so now they _____.
   a. are quiet   b. are being quiet

4. Don't eat that chocolate dessert. It _____.
   a. is not healthy   b. is not being healthy

5. Timmy! Those are bad words you're saying to Mr. Hawkes. You _____.
   a. are not polite   b. are not being polite

6. I'm worried about Jeff. He has pneumonia. He _____.
   a. is very ill   b. is being very ill

PRACTICE 8 ▸ Regular and irregular verbs. (Chart 1-4)
Part I. Read the passage. <u>Underline</u> the eight past tense verbs.

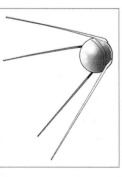

Sputnik

History <u>changed</u> on October 4th, 1957 when the Soviet Union successfully launched *Sputnik I.* The world's first artificial satellite was about the size of a beach ball (58 cm., or 22.8 in.), weighed only 83.6 kg., or 183.9 pounds, and took about 98 minutes to orbit the Earth on its elliptical path. That launch ushered in new political, military, technological, and scientific developments. While the *Sputnik* launch was a single event, it marked the start of the space age and the space race between the U.S. and the Soviet Union.

Part II. Answer the questions. Choose "T" if the statement is true. Choose "F" if the statement is false.

1. The Soviet Union launched the first artificial satellite.   (T)   F

2. The first satellite was about the size of a golf ball.   T   F

3. The first orbit around the Earth took about an hour and a half.   T   F

4. *Sputnik* went into space several times.   T   F

5. This first launch was the beginning of the space age and space race.   T   F

PRACTICE 9 ▸ Regular and irregular verbs. (Chart 1-4)
Complete the sentences. Write the simple past of the verbs in blue.

Part I. Regular verbs: The simple past ends in *–ed.*

1. It rains every afternoon in the summer. Yesterday it _____*rained*_____ all afternoon and all night too.

2. It snows a lot in Denver in the winter. Last January it _____ nearly every day.

3. I listen to the weather report every morning. Yesterday I _____ to the weather report several times.

Part II. Irregular verbs: The simple past does not end in *–ed.*

1. Lightening sometimes hits trees in this area. Last week a lightning bolt _____ my neighbor's tree and split it in half.

2. I usually wake up at 6:00 every morning, but today I _____ up at 4:00 because of a loud thunderstorm.

3. The sun rises in the morning. The sun _____ at 6:45 yesterday morning.

4. The sun sets in the evening. The sun _____ at 7:55 yesterday evening.

PRACTICE 10 ▸ Irregular verbs. (Chart 1-4)
Complete the sentences. Write the simple past tense of the verbs in blue.

1. Joe runs in marathons. Last year he _____*ran*_____ in the New York Marathon.

2. Athletes need to drink a lot of water. Joe _____ 12 glasses of water a day when he trained for the marathon.

3. Nowadays, I occasionally swim for exercise when I have time, but I _____ every day when I was a child.

4. Our basketball team doesn't win many games, but we _____ last Friday night.

5. Our soccer team didn't lose a single game this season until last night. Last night we _____ because we played so poorly.

6. Rhonda doesn't take many exercise classes now, but when she was younger she _____ karate and gymnastics classes.

7. The dance class usually begins at noon, but today the teacher was late. The class _____ ten minutes late.

8. Janice teaches a yoga class on Saturdays. Last Saturday she _____ two classes.

9. Harry goes to professional basketball games often. Last month he _____ to a Chicago Bulls game.

10. I always buy fresh vegetables on the weekend. Last Saturday I _____ fresh asparagus.

11. This year corn costs a lot more than it _____ last year.

12. Scott usually eats a salad for lunch. Yesterday he _____ a spinach salad.

13. Vanessa often gives me tomatoes from her garden. Last week she _____ me two baskets of tomatoes.

14. Margaret usually makes eggs for breakfast, but yesterday she _____ pancakes instead.

15. Yesterday I _____ sick, but today I feel much better.

PRACTICE 11 ▸ Irregular verbs. (Chart 1-4)
Write the simple past form of the verbs.

1. sell ___*sold*___	11. come _____	21. speak _____
2. buy _____	12. lose _____	22. go _____
3. begin _____	13. sleep _____	23. pay _____
4. have _____	14. build _____	24. forget _____
5. catch _____	15. fight _____	25. write _____
6. quit _____	16. understand _____	26. fall _____
7. find _____	17. spend _____	27. feel _____
8. make _____	18. let _____	28. leave _____
9. take _____	19. see _____	29. upset _____
10. break _____	20. teach _____	30. fly _____

PRACTICE 12 ▸ Irregular Verbs. (Chart 1-4)
In this exercise, a police reporter interviews the victim of a theft. The victim answers the questions, using a past tense verb. Write the victim's words.

1. REPORTER: So, a thief broke into your home last night?

   VICTIM: Yes, a thief _____*broke*_____ into my home last night.

2. REPORTER: Did he steal anything?

   VICTIM: Yes, he _____ some things.

3. REPORTER: Did you know he was in your apartment?

   VICTIM: Yes, I _____ he was in my apartment.

4. REPORTER: Did you hear him come in?

   VICTIM: Yes, I _____ him come in.

5. REPORTER: Did the police come?

   VICTIM: Yes, the police _____ .

6. REPORTER: Did your hands shake when you called the police?

   VICTIM: Yes, my hands _____ when I called them.

7. REPORTER: Did he hide in your garden?

   VICTIM: Yes, he _____ in my garden.

8. REPORTER: Did the police find him?

   VICTIM: Yes, the police _____ him.

9. REPORTER: Did they fight with him?

   VICTIM: Yes, they _____ with him.

10. REPORTER: Did he run away?

    VICTIM: Yes, he _____ away.

11. REPORTER: Did they shoot at him?

    VICTIM: Yes, they _____ at him.

12. REPORTER: Did they catch him?

    VICTIM: Yes, they _____ him.

PRACTICE 13 ▸ Simple past of irregular verbs. (Chart 1-4)

Complete the sentences. Write the simple past of the irregular verbs in the box. Pay special attention to spelling.

✓ bite	catch	hold	pay	sting
blow	feel	mean	quit	swim

1. I broke a tooth when I _____*bit*_____ into a piece of hard candy.

2. The little boy _____ his mother's hand as they walked toward the school bus.

3. Maria promised to help us. I hope she _____ what she said.

4. Arthur _____ out all of the candles on his birthday cake.

5. We both _____ eating fried foods months ago, and we already feel much better.

6. Douglas _____ the outside of his pocket to make sure his wallet was still there.

7. A bee _____ me on the hand while I was working in the garden.

8. Matthew Webb was the first person who _____ across the English Channel.

9. Paul _____ much more for his bike than I spent for mine.

10. Rita threw the ball high in the air. Daniel _____ it when it came down.

PRACTICE 14 ▸ Simple past of irregular verbs. (Chart 1-4)

Complete the sentences. Write the simple past form of the irregular verbs in the box. Pay special attention to spelling.

bet	fly	lead	sink	spin
choose	freeze	ring	✓ spend	weep

1. Dr. Perez _____ *spent* _____ ten hours in the operating room performing delicate surgery.

2. On my first day at the university, my English teacher _____ the class to our classroom. We all followed him.

3. Sally and I made a friendly bet. I _____ her that my grade on the math test would be higher than hers.

4. I _____ when I heard the tragic news. Everyone else cried too.

5. When I threw a piece of wood from the shore, it floated on top of the water. When I threw a rock, it _____ immediately to the bottom of the lake.

6. In 1927, Charles Lindbergh _____ from New York to Paris in 33 hours and 30 minutes.

7. When the children _____ around and around, they became dizzy.

8. The telephone _____ several times and then stopped before I could answer it.

9. William had trouble deciding which sweater he liked best, but he finally _____ the blue one.

10. The cold temperature _____ the water in the pond, so we can go ice-skating today.

PRACTICE 15 ▸ The simple past and the past progressive. (Chart 1-5)

Complete the sentences. Write the correct form of the verbs in parentheses.

1. Maria (*call*) _____ *called* _____ me as soon as she got the good news.

2. Last night at about nine o'clock we (*watch*) _____ TV when someone knocked at the door.

3. During the study period in class yesterday, it was hard for me to concentrate because the student next to me (*hum*) _____ .

4. When Harry (*meet*) _____ Janice, he immediately fell in love with her.

5. Jack was rushing to catch the bus when I (*see*) _____ him.

6. Last Saturday while Sandy (*clean*) _____ out the attic, she found her grandmother's wedding dress.

7. It started to rain while I (*drive*) _____ to work this morning. I didn't have an umbrella with me. I (*get*) _____ very wet when I stepped out of my car.

8. When we looked outside during the storm, we saw that the wind (*blow*) _____ very hard, and the trees (*bend*) _____ over in the wind.

9. When the teacher came into the room, most of the children (*play*) _____ together nicely. But over in the corner, Luke (*pull*) _____ Annie's hair. The teacher quickly ran over and pulled Luke away from Annie.

PRACTICE 16 ▸ The simple past and the past progressive. (Chart 1-5)
Write "1" before the action that started first. Write "2" before the action that started second.

1. When the alarm clock rang, I was sleeping.

   __2__ The alarm clock rang.

   __1__ I was sleeping.

2. When I saw Dr. Jarvis yesterday evening, he was waving at me.

   _____ I saw Dr. Jarvis yesterday evening.

   _____ He was waving at me.

3. When I saw Dr. Jarvis yesterday evening, he waved at me.

   _____ I saw Dr. Jarvis yesterday evening.

   _____ He waved at me.

4. I closed the windows when it was raining.

   _____ I closed the windows.

   _____ It began to rain.

5. I was closing the windows when it began to rain.

   _____ I was closing the windows.

   _____ It began to rain.

6. The server brought the check when we were eating our desserts.

   _____ The server brought the check.

   _____ We were eating our desserts.

7. When the doorbell rang, Sam went to the door. "Who is it?" he asked.

   _____ The doorbell rang.

   _____ Sam went to the door.

8. Sam was going to the door when the doorbell rang. "I'm coming, Bob," he said. "I saw you walking up the sidewalk."

   _____ The doorbell rang.

   _____ Sam was already going to the door.

PRACTICE 17 ▸ The simple past and the past progressive. (Chart 1-5)
Choose the correct completions.

1. We (had)/ were having   a wonderful dinner last night to celebrate our 25th wedding anniversary.

2. We   had / were having   a wonderful time when suddenly the electric power went out.

3. When Richard   stopped / was stopping   his car suddenly, the groceries   fell / were falling   out of the grocery bags and   spilled / were spilling   all over the floor of the car.

4. When I was a child, my mother always   served / was serving   cookies and milk to my friends and me when they   came / were coming   home with me after school.

5. When we   looked / were looking   in on our baby last night, he   slept / was sleeping.   I think he   dreamt / was dreaming   about something nice because he   smiled / was smiling.

6. A: Why is Henry in the hospital?

   B: He   worked / was working   on his car in the garage when the gas tank

      exploded / was exploding.

7. A: Oh! What   caused / was causing   the explosion?

   B: Henry   dropped / was dropping   a match too near the gas tank.

PRACTICE 18 ▸ Unfulfilled intentions. (Chart 1-6)
Complete each sentence with a logical phrase from the list. Write the letter of the phrase.

   a. it rained
   b. she didn't want to upset her
   c. I overslept this morning
   d. my battery died
   e. he was out of town
   f. her dinner guest is allergic to seafood
   g. there was no lettuce in the fridge
   h. it was too crowded

1. I was going to go to the library before class, but ___c___.

2. Jill was planning to invite Jeff to see a movie, but _____.

3. Susie was going to tell her sister the bad news, but _____.

4. Scott and Jeff were going to play baseball, but _____.

5. I was going to text you, but _____.

6. Lesley was going to make a salad, but _____.

7. Joy was going to cook lobster, but _____.

8. We were going to go to the new restaurant, but _____.

PRACTICE 19 ▸ Unfulfilled intentions. (Chart 1-6)
Check (✓) the sentences that you can rewrite with **was planning** for the underlined words.

1. a. __✓__ I was going to wash my car, but it started to rain.

   b. _____ I was washing my car when it began to rain.

   c. _____ I was going to the store when I remembered that my wallet was at home.

2. a. _____ We were going to visit our cousins, but Jack got sick.

   b. _____ We were going to see them tomorrow.

   c. _____ We were going to our cousins, but we had car trouble.

3. a. _____ Were you going to come to the meeting?

   b. _____ Were we meeting at 1:00?

   c. _____ Were you going home after the meeting?

PRACTICE 20 ▸ Chapter review.

Underline the verbs. Decide which of the following phrases best describes the action of each sentence. Write the appropriate number.

1. actions occurring now or today
2. habitual / everyday actions
3. actions completed in the past (non-progressive)
4. one action in progress when another occurred

1. __2__ I take the bus to school when it rains.

2. __4__ I was riding the bus when I heard the news on my radio.

3. _____ I am riding the bus because my friend is repairing my bike.

4. _____ I rode the bus home yesterday because you forgot to pick me up.

5. _____ Dennis was having coffee this morning when a bird crashed into his kitchen window.

6. _____ Dennis had a big breakfast, but his wife didn't eat anything.

7. _____ Dennis is having a big breakfast this morning.

8. _____ Dennis generally has coffee with breakfast.

9. _____ My mother and I celebrate our birthdays together because they are just a few days apart.

10. _____ We were working when you called on our birthdays last week.

11. _____ One year we celebrated our birthdays apart because my mom was away on business.

PRACTICE 21 ▸ Chapter review.

Complete the crossword puzzle. Use the clues under the puzzle. Write the correct form of the verbs in parentheses.

Across

2. Shhh. I'm (*listen*) _____ to the radio.

5. Good idea! I (*think*) _____ your suggestion is great.

7. What was that? I just (*hear*) _____ a loud noise.

8. I am (*think*) _____ about going home early today.

Down

1. We (*go*) _____ to Mexico last year.

3. I was in my room (*study*) _____ when you called.

4. I (*eat*) _____ lunch with friends yesterday.

6. This is fun. I'm (*have*) _____ a great time here.

7. I only (*have*) _____ a little money right now.

PRACTICE 22 ▸ Chapter review.

Complete the sentences with the correct form of the verbs in parentheses.

A hurricane (*be*) ___*is*___ a huge tropical storm. It brings very strong winds and
                   1
heavy rain. Hurricanes (*form*) _____ over large bodies of warm water.
                                        2
They (*gather*) _____ heat and energy from warm water. Hurricanes
                        3
(*rotate*) _____ around the center of the storm, called the "eye." The eye of
                  4
a hurricane (*be*) _____ the calmest part of the storm. A hurricane usually
                          5
(*last*) _____ for over a week and (*move*) _____ 10–20 miles
             6   7
per hour over the open water. Hurricanes typically (*grow*) _____ weak over land,
                                                                      8
but when they first touch land, the heavy rain and strong winds (*damage*) _____
                                                                                    9
buildings and trees. These storms sometimes (*destroy*) _____ coastal towns.
                                                               10

One of the most damaging hurricanes to hit the United States was Hurricane Katrina in
August, 2005. Hurricane Katrina (*form*) _____ over the Bahamas. Then it
                                               11
(*move*) _____ to Florida and crossed the Gulf Coast. It (*cost*) _____
              12   13
billions of dollars in property damage. It especially (*cause*) _____ damage to the city of
                                                                 14
New Orleans. By the end of the storm, about 80% of the city (*be*) _____ underwater.
                                                                         15
While the storm (*approach*) _____, many residents (*try*) _____
                                    16   17
unsuccessfully to leave the city. It (*be*) _____ one of the deadliest and costliest hurricanes in
                                             18
U.S. history.

There is still a lot to learn about hurricanes. Today scientists (*study*) _____
                                                                                 19
ways to better predict a hurricane's path. City planners (*learn*) _____ more about
                                                                          20
preparation for hurricanes. Architects and engineers (*discover*) _____ better ways
                                                                           21
to design stronger homes and buildings. Better preparation is the best protection against these deadly
storms.

PRACTICE 23 ▶ Chapter review.

There is one verb error in each sentence. Correct the error.

1. Carole ~~visit~~ *visits* India every year.

2. In the past, no one was caring about air pollution.

3. Today we are knowing that air pollution is a serious health and environmental problem.

4. I move to Houston two years ago.

5. I was eating dinner when you call.

6. The students taking a test right now.

7. Judy felt on the slippery floor.

8. I was going to transferred to another university, but I decided to stay here.

Perfect and Perfect Progressive Tenses

PRACTICE 1 ▶ Preview.

Part I. Read the passage.

> ### Ride-Sharing Companies
>
> Ride-sharing companies have become some of the world's largest taxi companies, but they don't own any actual taxis. When customers need a driver, they submit their request through the company's app. The drivers use their own cars. Uber is one example of a ride-sharing company. Uber first began in San Francisco in 2009. By 2012, the company had expanded into several major U.S. cities, such as New York, Chicago, and Washington, D.C. Since that time, it has been expanding internationally. Today, people in countries all over the world use ride-sharing companies. While many people have praised these companies, others have expressed concerns over the safety of the ride-sharing system.

1. Write the 7 verbs in the simple present tense.

   _____

2. Write the 3 verbs in the present perfect tense.

   _____

3. Write the verb in the present perfect progressive tense.

   _____

4. Write the verb in the simple past tense.

   _____

5. Write the verb in the past perfect tense.

   _____

Part II. Answer the questions. Choose "T" if the statement is true. Choose "F" if the statement is false.

1. The world's largest taxi companies don't have traditional taxis.   T   F

2. Uber expanded into New York in 2009.   T   F

3. Uber had drivers in Chicago before it expanded internationally.   T   F

4. Customers use an app to find drivers.   T   F

PRACTICE 2 ▸ Irregular verbs. (Charts 2-1 and 2-2)
Complete the chart.

Simple Form	Simple Past	Past Participle
1.	shut	
2. bring		
3.		heard
4.	lost	
5. teach		
6.		begun
7. sing		
8.	ate	
9. see		
10.	threw	
11. become		
12. go		

PRACTICE 3 ▸ The present perfect. (Chart 2-3)
Complete each sentence with *for* or *since*.

1. I haven't seen Elvira …

   a. _____ several years.

   b. _____ a long time.

   c. _____ the holiday last year.

   d. _____ she was in college.

   e. _____ more than a month.

   f. _____ she got married.

   g. _____ she became famous.

2. Mehdi and Pat have been friends …

   a. _____ they were in college.

   b. _____ about 20 years.

   c. _____ 2005.

   d. _____ a long time.

   e. _____ they began to work together.

   f. _____ they met.

   g. _____ their entire adult lives.

PRACTICE 4 ▶ The present perfect with *since*, *for*, and *ago*. (Chart 2-3)
Complete the sentences with the correct time expression.

1. Today is the 21st of April. I started this job on April 1st. I started this job
   _____*three weeks*_____ ago. I have had this job since _____*April 1st*_____.
   I have had this job for _____*three weeks*_____.

2. I made a New Year's resolution on January 1st: I will get up at 6:00 A.M. every day instead
   of 7:00 A.M. Today is March 1st, and I have gotten up every morning at 6:00 A.M. I made
   this resolution _____ ago. I have gotten up at 6:00 A.M. since
   _____. I have gotten up at 6:00 A.M. for _____.

3. Today is February 28th. Valentine's Day was on February 14th. I sent my girlfriend some
   chocolates on Valentine's Day, and she texted me a "Thank you." After that, I did not hear from her
   again. I have not heard from her for _____. I have not heard from her
   since _____.

4. Today is January 27th, 2016. Sue works for Senator Brown. She began to work for him right after she
   first met him in January, 2010. She began to work for Senator Brown _____
   ago. Sue has worked for Senator Brown for _____. She has worked for
   Senator Brown since _____.

PRACTICE 5 ▶ The present perfect with *since* and *for*. (Chart 2-3)
Rewrite the sentences using ***since*** and ***for***.

1. We know Mrs. Jones. We met her last month.
   a. for _____*We have known Mrs. Jones for one month.*_____
   b. since _____

2. They live in New Zealand. They moved there in 2014.
   a. for _____
   b. since _____

3. I like foreign films. I liked them five years ago.
   a. since _____
   b. for _____

4. Jack works for a software company. He started working there last year.
   a. for _____
   b. since _____

PRACTICE 6 ▶ The present perfect. (Charts 2-3 and 2-4)

Complete the sentences using the present perfect tense. Write the correct past participle of the verbs in blue.

1. I often eat Thai food. I have _____ Thai food three times this week.

2. I sometimes visit my cousins on weekends. I have _____ them twice this month.

3. I work at the Regional Bank. I have _____ there for eleven years.

4. I like card games. I have _____ card games since I was a child.

5. I know Professor Blonsky. She's my next-door neighbor. I have _____ her all my life.

6. I wear glasses. I have _____ glasses since I was ten years old.

7. I take piano lessons. I have _____ piano lessons for several years.

8. I go to Unisex Haircutters once a month. I have _____ to the same shop for twenty years.

PRACTICE 7 ▶ The present perfect. (Charts 2-3 and 2-4)

Complete the sentences with the present perfect tense of the appropriate verb in the box. Use each verb only once. Include any words in parentheses.

✓ eat	know	ride	sweep	win
improve	make	start	swim	write

1. A: How about more pie?

   B: No, but thanks. I can't swallow another bite. I (already) _____*have already eaten*_____ too much.

2. Our football team is having a great season. They _____ all but one of their games so far this year and will probably win the championship.

3. Jane is expecting a letter from me, but I (not) _____ to her yet. Maybe I'll call her instead.

4. Jack is living in Spain now. His Spanish used to be terrible, but it _____ greatly since he moved there.

5. A: Let's hurry! I think the movie is beginning!

   B: No, the movie (not) _____ yet. They're just showing previews of the coming attractions.

6. A: I hear your parents are coming to visit you. Is that why you're cleaning your apartment?

   B: You guessed it! I (already) _____ the floor, but I still need to dust the furniture. Want to help?

7. A: I understand Tom is a good friend of yours? How long (you) _____ him?

   B: Since we were kids.

8. Everyone makes mistakes in life. I _____ lots of mistakes in my life. The important thing is to learn from one's mistakes. Right?

9. A: I (never) _____ on the subways in New York City. Have you?

   B: I've never even been to New York City.

10. A: (you, ever) _____ in the Atlantic Ocean?

    B: No, only the Pacific — when I was in Hawaii. I even went snorkeling when I was there.

PRACTICE 8 ▸ The present perfect. (Charts 2-2 → 2-4)

Choose the correct sentence.

1. a. Scott has always wanted to go scuba diving. He's been snorkeling, but he hasn't tried scuba diving yet.
   b. Scott has always wanted to go scuba diving. He's been snorkeling, but he hasn't tried scuba diving never.

2. a. Kevin is jittery. He's yet had seven cups of coffee this morning. He should avoid drinking any more caffeine today.
   b. Kevin is jittery. He's already had seven cups of coffee this morning. He should avoid drinking any more caffeine today.

3. a. Vanessa has tried on five different dresses, but she still hasn't found the right one.
   b. Vanessa has tried on five different dresses, but she already hasn't found the right one.

4. a. I wish our professor would give us a break. This is only the third week of class, and we've ever written five essays.
   b. I wish our professor would give us a break. This is only the third week of class, and we've already written five essays.

5. a. We need to write twelve essays this semester. We've wrote only five so far.
   b. We need to write twelve essays this semester. We've written only five so far.

6. a. I haven't had time to finish my research paper yet.
   b. I haven't have time to finish my research paper yet.

7. a. Have you ever been to Shanghai?
   b. Haven't you never been to Shanghai?

8. a. I've ever been to China, but I hope I can go there some day.
   b. I've never been to China, but I hope I can go there some day.

9. a. I wish I could get over this cold. I've had it ever since the beginning of the semester.
   b. I wish I could get over this cold. I've had it never since the beginning of the semester.

10. a. I've gone to the doctor twice, but I didn't get better yet.
    b. I've gone to the doctor twice, but I haven't gotten better yet.

11. a. I've never tried homeopathic medicine, but my neighbor says it's great.
    b. I haven't never tried homeopathic medicine, but my neighbor says it's great.

12. a. I hope I didn't fail my chemistry test. It was the most difficult exam I've ever taken.
    b. I hope I didn't fail my chemistry test. It was the most difficult exam I've still taken.

PRACTICE 9 ▸ *Is* vs. *has.* (Chart 2-5)

In spoken English, *is* and *has* can both be contracted to *'s*. Decide if the verb in the contraction is *is* or *has*.

Spoken English	Written English
1. He's absent.	_____
2. Sue's been a nurse for a long time.	_____
3. Her brother's in the hospital.	_____
4. He's not happy.	_____
5. He's felt bad this past week.	_____
6. Here is a newspaper. Take one. It's free.	_____
7. The manager's taken some money.	_____
8. Mira's taking a break.	_____
9. Mira's taken a break.	_____

PRACTICE 10 ▸ The present perfect and the simple past. (Chart 2-6)
Choose the correct completions.

1. a. Botswana   became / has become   an independent country in 1966.

   b. Botswana   was / has been   an independent country for more than 40 years.

2. a. It's raining. It   was / has been   raining since noon today.

   b. It's raining. It's the rainy season. It   rained / has rained   every day since the first of the month.

3. a. I grew up in Scotland until I moved to Argentina with my family. I was 12 then. Now I am 21.
   I   lived / have lived   in Scotland for 12 years.

   b. Now I live in Argentina. I   lived / have lived   in Argentina for 9 years.

4. a. Claude and Pierre worked together at the French restaurant for 30 years. They retired three
   years ago. They   worked / have worked   together for 30 years.

   b. Claude and Pierre   didn't work / haven't worked   for the last three years.

PRACTICE 11 ▸ The present perfect and the simple past. (Chart 2-6)
Complete the sentences with the correct form of the verbs in parentheses.

1. (*know*) I _____*knew*_____ Tim when he was a child, but I haven't seen him for many
   years. I _____*have known*_____ Larry, my best friend, for more than 20 years.

2. (*agree*) The company and its employees finally _____ on salary raises
   two days ago. Since then, they _____ on everything, and the rest of the
   negotiations have gone smoothly.

3. (*take*) Mark _____ a trip to Asia last October. He _____
   many trips to Asia since he started his own import-export business.

4. (*play*) Ivan _____ the violin at several concerts with the London Symphony
   since 1990. Last year he _____ Beethoven's violin concerto at one of the
   concerts.

5. (*call*) When she was in college, Julia _____ her parents a few times a week.
   Now she has a job and is living in Chicago. In the last month she _____ her
   parents only three times.

6. (*send*) Our university _____ 121 students to study in other countries last
   year. In total, we _____ 864 students abroad over the last ten years.

7. (*fly*) Masaru is a pilot for JAL. He _____ nearly 8 million miles during the
   last 22 years. Last year he _____ 380,000 miles.

8. (*oversleep*) Mark missed his physics examination this morning because he _____.
   He _____ a lot since the beginning of the semester. He needs to buy a new
   alarm clock.

PRACTICE 12 ▸ The present perfect and the present perfect progressive. (Chart 2-7)
Choose the correct completions.

1. Sam and Judy began talking on the phone at 9:00 P.M. Now it is 11:00 P.M., and they are still talking. They   have talked / have been talking   for two hours.

2. Sam and Judy speak to each other on the phone several times a day. They are speaking on the phone now, and they might speak again later. Today they   have spoken / have been speaking   to each other on the phone at least seven times.

3. England   has won / has been winning   the World Cup only once since 1930.

4. How long   have you sat / have you been sitting   here in the sun? You're very red. You need to get out of the sun.

5. The chair in the president's office is very special. Sixteen presidents   have sat / have been sitting   in it.

PRACTICE 13 ▸ The present perfect and the present perfect progressive. (Chart 2-7)
Complete the sentences. Write either the present perfect or the present perfect progressive of the verbs in parentheses.

1. The kids are at the park. They (*play*) _____ *have been playing* _____ ball for the last two hours, but they don't seem tired yet.

2. Jim (*play*) _____ *has played* _____ soccer only a couple of times, so he's not very good at it. He's much better at tennis.

3. Karl (*raise*) _____ three children to adulthood. Now they are educated and working in productive careers.

4. Katie is falling asleep at her desk. Dr. Wu (*lecture*) _____ since ten o'clock, and it's now past noon.

5. Jenna is a law student. Ever since she enrolled in law school, she
   (*miss, never*) _____ a class because of illness.

6. Tim (*sleep*) _____ in the downstairs bedroom only once. He usually sleeps upstairs in the bedroom he shares with his brother.

7. A: How much longer until we arrive at the Singapore airport?
   B: Let me see. It's about 9:15. We (*fly*) _____ for almost six hours. We will be there in another couple of hours.

8. Janice (*sleep*) _____ for almost eleven hours. Do you want me to wake her up?

9. A: Is the rescue crew still looking for survivors of the plane crash?
   B: Yes, they (*search*) _____ the area for hours, but they haven't found anybody else.

PRACTICE 14 ▶ Simple past vs. the present perfect progressive. (Chart 2-7)
Look at the information about Janet and write sentences with the given words. Use the simple past or present perfect progressive as necessary.

In 1998, Janet received her English teaching degree. Here is what happened to Janet after that:

1999	2000	2001	now
move to Canada	join Lingua Schools as a teaching assistant	become a teacher	be a teacher

1. (move to Canada) _____ *In 1999, Janet moved to Canada.* _____

2. (join Lingua Schools) _____

3. (be a teacher) _____

4. (teach her own class) _____

5. (work at Lingua Schools) _____

PRACTICE 15 ▶ The present perfect, the present perfect progressive, and the past perfect. (Charts 2-3 → 2-8)
Read the two reviews for a smart phone. Choose the correct completions.

***** Best phone ever!

1. Before I purchased this item, I   have / have had   the same phone for over five years. I
   had been thinking / am thinking   about upgrading for years, but I really liked my old phone. I had
   also   been worried / worry   about learning to use such complicated technology. Actually, I had
   nothing to worry about. This phone is so easy to use! I   've had / 've been having   it for only three
   weeks, and I've already learned how to use all the major features. I've installed several apps, and the
   phone still has a lot of memory. I have a terrible sense of direction, and the built-in GPS
   has been / had been   a lifesaver. My favorite feature is the camera. I've already   took / taken
   hundreds of pictures. The picture quality is amazing. This is the best purchase I've ever made!

***** Buyers beware!

2. The price is right. That is the only good thing I can say about this phone. My friends
   had warned / have been warning   me that you get what you pay for, but I didn't listen. Now I have
   a piece of junk. For the past two months it   has given / gave   me nothing but problems. Ever
   since I installed my favorite photo-editing software, the phone   is crashing / has been crashing
   daily. When I try to open more than two apps, the screen freezes. It has been driving me crazy!
   The camera on this phone is terrible. I   've taken / 'd taken   better pictures on my old phone.
   There are much better products available.

PRACTICE 16 ▶ The simple past and the past perfect. (Charts 1-5 and 2-8)

Underline each event. Write "1" over the event that happened first and "2" over the event that happened second.

               1   *2*

1. <u>We had driven only two miles</u> when <u>we got a flat tire.</u>

2. Alan told me that he had written a book.

3. By the time we arrived at the airport, the plane had already left.

4. The dog had eaten the entire roast before anyone knew it was gone.

5. We didn't stand in line for tickets because we had already bought them by mail.

6. Carl played the guitar so well because he had studied with a famous guitarist.

7. By the time the movie ended, everyone had fallen asleep.

8. After the professor had corrected the third paper, he was exhausted from writing comments on the students' papers.

9. I had just placed an order at the store for a new camera when I found a cheaper one online.

PRACTICE 17 ▶ The past perfect. (Chart 2-8)

Complete the sentences. Write the correct form of the past perfect.

1. Yesterday, John got 100% on a math exam. Before yesterday, he (*get, not*) _____ 100%.

2. Last week, Sonya met her fiancé's parents. Before that, she (*meet, not*) _____ them.

3. Caroline went to a Japanese restaurant today. Before today, she (*try, never*) _____ sushi.

4. A few days ago, Bakir cooked a frozen dinner. Before that, he (*eat, not*) _____ a frozen dinner.

5. Last week, I had to have a tooth pulled. Until then, I (*have, not*) _____ any problems with my teeth.

PRACTICE 18 ▶ The simple past and the past perfect. (Charts 1-5 and 2-8)

Complete the sentences with the simple past or past perfect form of the verb. Write the letter of the correct verb.

1. By the time Jason arrived to help, we _____ moving everything.
   a. already finished   b. had already finished

2. The apartment was hot when I got home, so I _____ the air conditioner.
   a. turned on   b. had turned on

3. The farmer's barn caught on fire some time during the night. By the time the firefighters arrived, the building _____ to the ground. It was a total loss.
   a. burned   b. had burned

4. The dinner I had at that restaurant was expensive! Until then, I _____ so much on one meal.
   a. never spent   b. had never spent

5. When I saw that Mike was having trouble, I _____ him. He was very appreciative.
   a. helped   b. had helped

6. My wife and I went to Disneyland when we visited Los Angeles last spring. Before that time, we

   _____ such a big amusement park. It was a lot of fun.
   a. never visited   b. had never visited

7. My flight to Australia took a long time. I _____ on airplanes for fairly long distances before, but not
   as long as that trip.
   a. traveled   b. had traveled

PRACTICE 19 ▸ The simple past and the past perfect. (Charts 1-5 and 2-8)
Write the simple past or the past perfect of the verbs in parentheses. In some cases, both forms are correct.

1. Yesterday I (go) _____went_____ to my daughter's dance recital.

   I (be, never) _____had never been_____ to a dance recital before.

   I (take, not) _____didn't take_____ dancing lessons when I (be) _____was_____ a child.

2. Last night, I (eat) _____ four servings of food at the "all-you-can-eat" special

   dinner at The Village Restaurant. Until that time, I (eat, never) _____ so much in

   one meal. I've felt miserable all day today.

3. A: I (see) _____ you in the school play last night. You (do) _____ a

      terrific acting job. (you, act, ever) _____ in a play before this one?

   B: Yes. I (start) _____ acting when I was in elementary school.

PRACTICE 20 ▸ The present perfect progressive and the past perfect progressive.
(Charts 2-7 and 2-10)
Choose the correct completions.

1. I'm studying English. I   have been studying / had been studying   English for several years now.

2. I came from Malaysia to live in New Zealand in 2002. I   have been studying / had been studying

   English for three years before that.

3. Shhh! I want to see the end of this TV show! I   have been waiting / had been waiting   to find out

   who the murderer is.

4. Laura finally called me last night. I hadn't heard from her in four months. I

   have been waiting / had been waiting   for that call for a long time!

5. Before Ada became a veterinarian last year, she   has been working / had been working

   as a veterinarian's assistant while she was in school.

6. Li is going to quit his job. He   has been working / had been working   too many hours for too little

   money in this job. He is probably going to resign next week.

PRACTICE 21 ▶ The present perfect progressive and the past perfect progressive.
(Charts 2-7 and 2-10)

Complete the sentences. Write the present perfect progressive or the past perfect progressive form of the verbs in parentheses.

1. Anna (*listen*) _____*had been listening*_____ to loud rock music when her friends arrived, but she turned it off so all of them could study together. When they finished, she turned it back on, and now they (*dance*) _____*have been dancing*_____ and (*sing*) _____*singing*_____ for two hours.

2. We (*wait*) _____ for Ali for the last two hours, but he still hasn't arrived.

3. We (*wait*) _____ for Ali for over three hours before he finally arrived yesterday.

4. Oscar (*train*) _____ for the Olympics for the last three years and wants to make the national team next year.

5. The marathon runner (*run*) _____ for almost two hours when he collapsed on the pavement. He received immediate medical attention.

6. Tom had a hard time finding a job. He (*try*) _____ to get a new job for six months before he finally found a position at a local community college. Now he has a two-year contract. He (*teach*) _____ there for only a few weeks, but he likes his new job very much.

7. Dr. Sato (*perform*) _____ specialized surgery since she began working at the university hospital ten years ago. She still does many operations each year, but now her work is very famous, and she travels all over the world lecturing to other surgeons on her technique.

PRACTICE 22 ▶ Chapter review.

There is one verb error in each sentence. Correct the error.

1. *Citizen Kane* is a great classic movie. I've been seeing it ten times.

2. *War and Peace* is a long novel. I'm reading it for two months, and I am still not finished with it!

3. Our guests have left yesterday.

4. We were studying all night. Let's take a break now.

5. Let's not leave yet. I'd been having such a wonderful time at this party.

6. By the time I got home, the rest of the family has eaten.

7. I was late for my nine o'clock class, so I had run all the way from my dorm to my class.

8. Mrs. Wang isn't in the hospital anymore. She had left early this morning.

9. I was born on February 29th in 1960, a leap year. February 29th occurs only once every four years. So by the time the 21st century began, I celebrated only ten birthdays!

10. A: Are you still on the phone? Are you holding on for someone?

    B: Yes, I am. I am still holding for the technical support department. I am holding for more than half an hour!

CHAPTER 3

Future Time

PRACTICE 1 ▸ Preview.

Part I. Read the passage. <u>Underline</u> the seven verb forms with **will**.

> **Yellowstone National Park**
>
> Welcome to your ski vacation at Yellowstone National Park! According to the weather forecast, you will have plenty of fresh snow to enjoy this weekend. Before you begin your ski adventure, you need to be aware of possible dangerous situations.
>
> First, make sure you dress appropriately. Temperatures can rise and fall dramatically. Dressing in layers will help you avoid hypothermia and frostbite. A light inner layer of clothing will keep you comfortable and dry. A middle layer will help your body stay warm, and a waterproof outer layer will protect you against rain or snow.
>
> Second, you may encounter wild animals on the trails, but do not approach or try to feed them. You will scare them, and they may become aggressive. In general, animals won't bother you if you don't bother them.
>
> Finally, study a trail map of the ski area so you don't get lost. Stay safe and enjoy your time here!

Part II. Answer the questions. Choose "T" if the statement is true. Choose "F" if the statement is false.

1. The weather forecast predicts good conditions for skiing.   T   F

2. You won't need to dress in layers if the temperature is high.   T   F

3. Animals won't become aggressive if you feed them.   T   F

4. Most animals are always aggressive even if you don't approach them.   T   F

5. Trail maps help you stay safe.   T   F

PRACTICE 2 ▸ Simple future: *be going to*. (Chart 3-1)
Complete the sentences with the correct form of **be going to** and the verbs in parentheses.

1. Vanessa and Ben (*travel*) _____ to France next summer.

2. They (*tour*) _____ Paris.

3. They (*visit*) _____ the Louvre, the Eiffel Tower, and the Arc de Triomphe.

4. Ben (*take*) _____ an intensive French class at a language school in Paris.

5. He (*study*) _____ French five hours a day for three weeks.

6. Vanessa is a doctor. She (*do*) _____ volunteer work for the French Red Cross for two weeks.

7. They (*return*) _____ home at the end of the summer.

PRACTICE 3 ▸ Simple future: *will* and *be going to*. (Chart 3-1)

Complete the sentences in two ways. Write sentence "a." with ***will*** and sentence "b." with ***be going to***. Use the correct verb in the box.

| arrive | bloom | buy | end | rain | set | take |

1. a. The sun rose at 5:46 this morning, and it _____ at 6:52 tonight.

   b. The sun rose at 5:46 this morning, and it _____ at 6:52 tonight.

2. a. The flight left Bangkok at noon today, and it _____ in Mumbai at midnight.

   b. The flight left Bangkok at noon today, and it _____ in Mumbai at midnight.

3. a. There are dark clouds over the mountain. It _____ later today.

   b. There are dark clouds over the mountain. It _____ later today.

4. a. We planted the flowers in March, and they _____ in June.

   b. We planted the flowers in March, and they _____ in June.

5. a. Our semester began in January, and it _____ in May.

   b. Our semester began in January, and it _____ in May.

6. a. When _____ you _____ a new computer?

   b. When _____ you _____ a new computer?

7. a. I _____ not _____ a vacation this year. Maybe next year.

   b. I _____ not _____ a vacation this year. Maybe next year.

PRACTICE 4 ▸ Simple future: *will* and *be going to*. (Chart 3-1)

Part I. Read the message from a history professor to her students.

The History 101 final exam will be next Friday from 9:00 till 11:00. You need to study the first 12 chapters of the textbook. You do not need to study Chapters 13 and 14. Please review the first part of Chapter 15. The rest of that chapter is not important for your exam. Be prepared to answer a total of 50 multiple-choice questions. Unlike your other exams, you will not have any essay questions on the final. Grades will be available a week after the exam.

Part II. Complete the sentences with ***is, isn't, are, aren't, will,*** or ***won't***.

1. The students in History 101 _____ going to take a final exam next week.

2. The students _____ have two hours to take the exam.

3. The exam _____ going to cover the first 12 chapters and part of Chapter 15.

4. Chapters 13 and 14 _____ going to be on the exam.

5. The second part of Chapter 15 _____ going to be on the exam.

6. The test _____ going to consist of multiple-choice questions.

7. There _____ be any essay questions.

8. Students _____ get their grades a week after the exam.

PRACTICE 5 ▶ *Will* vs. *be going to.* (Chart 3-2)

Check (✓) the box that describes each sentence.

	Prediction	Prior Plan	Willingness
1. I'll help you change your tire, Ms. Olsen.			✓
2. It's going to rain tomorrow.			
3. It will rain tomorrow.			
4. Louise is going to help us next week.			
5. Wait. I'll help you carry your luggage.			
6. We're going to see a movie tonight.			

PRACTICE 6 ▶ *Will* vs. *be going to.* (Chart 3-2)

Choose "a." if the meaning describes a prior plan. Choose "b." if the meaning describes a decision of the moment.

1. I can't have lunch with you on Friday because I'm going to meet with my professor at noon.
   a. prior plan   b. decision of the moment

2. My computer just crashed. I'll call the technical support department to fix it right now.
   a. prior plan   b. decision of the moment

3. It's very icy and slippery on my street this morning. I'll go out and clear the sidewalk.
   a. prior plan   b. decision of the moment

4. Roberto and Sandy are going to get married next Saturday.
   a. prior plan   b. decision of the moment

5. Jimmy is going to have a tonsillectomy on Monday. The doctors are going to take out his tonsils.
   a. prior plan   b. decision of the moment

6. Look at the price of the airport limousine. It's too much money. We'll go by bus.
   a. prior plan   b. decision of the moment

PRACTICE 7 ▶ *Will* vs. *be going to.* (Chart 3-2)

Choose the correct response(s) to the questions or statements. More than one response may be correct.

1. A: What about Dominick? Doesn't he want to come with us?

   B: Nobody knows!   I'll call / I'm going to call   him tonight to find out.

2. A: Jessica practices her violin for ten hours a day!

   B: I know!   She's going to be / She'll be   a famous violinist some day.

3. A: How about dinner and a movie on Friday?

   B: Sorry, I can't.   I'm going to fly / I'll fly   to London on Friday evening.

4. A: Do you and Paul have tickets for any of the hockey games this season?

   B: Yes, we do.   We're going to go to the game / We'll go to the game   tomorrow night.

5. A: I can't open this jar!

   B: Give it to me.   I'm going to open it / I'll open it   for you.

6. A: So you're leaving to go to another university, Professor Hu!

   B: Yes,   I'm going to teach / I will teach   at Emory University. They've made me a great offer.

PRACTICE 8 ▸ Will vs. be going to. (Chart 3-2)

Complete the sentences with **will** or **be going to**. Include any words in parentheses.

1. A: Excuse me, waiter! This isn't what I ordered. I ordered a chicken salad.

   B: Sorry, sir. I _____*will*_____ take this back and get your salad.

   A: Thank you.

2. A: Would you like to join Linda and me tomorrow? We _____*are going to*_____ visit the natural history museum.

   B: Sure. I've never been there.

3. A: Where's the mustard?

   B: In the refrigerator, on the middle shelf.

   A: I've looked there.

   B: OK. I _____ get it for you.

4. A: What's all this paint for? (*you*) _____ paint your house?

   B: No, we _____ paint my mother's house.

5. A: Paul, do you want to go to the mall with me?

   B: No thanks. I already have plans. I _____ wash my car and then clean out the basement.

6. A: Someone needs to take this report to Mr. Day's office right away, but I can't leave my desk.

   B: I _____ do it.

   A: Thanks.

7. A: Who'll pick up Uncle Jack at the airport?

   B: I _____.

8. A: Why is Carlos wearing a suit and tie? He usually wears jeans to class.

   B: He _____ give a speech at the faculty lunch today.

9. A: Let me ask you something, Toshi.

   B: Sure. What's up, Andy?

   A: I _____ interview for a job this afternoon, and ... well, do I need a tie? I don't have a decent one.

   B: Yes, you need a tie. I _____ lend you one of mine.

   A: Thanks.

10. A: You're going out?

    B: Yes. I _____ stop at the grocery store for some fruit and some rice. Can you think of anything else we need?

    A: How about getting some chocolate-covered nuts?

    B: Good idea! I _____ get some of those too.

PRACTICE 9 ▶ Expressing the future in time clauses. (Chart 3-3)
Complete the sentences with the correct form of the verbs in parentheses.

1. Grandma and Grandpa are planning to travel often when they (*retire*) _____.
2. I'll wake up tomorrow morning when the alarm clock (*ring*) _____.
3. The students will relax after they (*finish*) _____ their final exams.
4. You'll feel a lot better after you (*take*) _____ this medicine.
5. The residents of the coastal areas will prepare for the hurricane before it (*arrive*) _____.
6. Mark will work in a law firm as soon as he (*graduate*) _____ from law school.
7. We'll have dinner as soon as the rice (*be*) _____ ready.
8. I'll tell you as soon I (*hear*) _____ any news.
9. Before we (*leave*) _____ on vacation, we'll stop our newspaper delivery.
10. We'll start our newspaper delivery again after we (*get*) _____ back from vacation.

PRACTICE 10 ▶ Expressing the future in time clauses. (Chart 3-3)
Complete each sentence with the correct clause from Column A or Column B.

	Column A	**Column B**
1. When I see Irina later, _b_.	a. I give her the news	b. I'll give her the news
2. I'll call you tomorrow _____.	a. after I talk to Rita	b. after I will talk to Rita
3. As soon as I hear from Tom, _____.	a. I call you	b. I'll call you
4. We'll all be very happy _____.	a. when you get here	b. when you will get here
5. I'll save my files _____.	a. before I shut down my computer	b. before I will shut down my computer
6. The passengers will get off the plane _____.	a. after it lands	b. after it is going to land
7. My cell phone won't work _____.	a. until I unlock it	b. until I will unlock it
8. After the party is over tonight, _____.	a. we call a taxi to go home	b. we'll call a taxi to go home
9. I'm not going to pay for the refrigerator _____.	a. until they fix the broken door	b. until they will fix the broken door
10. I'll take this new medicine _____.	a. before I go to bed tonight	b. before I will go to bed tonight

PRACTICE 11 ▶ Expressing the future in time clauses. (Chart 3-3)
Complete the sentences with the following: the simple present, the future with ***will,*** or the future with a form of ***be going to.*** In some sentences, both ***will*** and ***be going to*** may be possible.

1. The strike has been going on for over two months now. The strikers (*return, not*)
   _____*will not / are not going to return*_____ to work until they (*get*) ___*get*___ a raise and the
   benefits they are demanding.

2. When Rita (*get*) _____ her driver's license next week, she
   (*be*) _____ able to drive to school every day.

3. A: Mr. Jackson called. He'll be here at the garage to pick up his car in a few minutes. He

(be, not) _____ very happy when he (learn) _____ about the

bill for repairs on his car. Do you want to talk to him when he (come) _____ in

and (ask) _____ about his bill?

B: Not especially, but I will.

4. After Ali (return) _____ to his country next month, he

(work) _____ at the Ministry of Agriculture.

5. According to the newspaper, the Department of Transportation

(build) _____ a new four-lane highway into the city

next year. In my opinion, it (be) _____ outdated before they

(complete) _____ it. We need a six-lane highway.

6. A: Have you heard any news about Barbara since her car accident?

B: No, I've heard nothing. As soon as I (hear) _____ something, I

(let) _____ you know.

7. A: I see you're reading *The Silk Road*.

B: I (lend) _____ it to you as soon as I (finish) _____ it.

A: Really? Thanks!

8. A: Relax. The plumber is on his way. He (be) _____ here before long to

fix that leak in the pipe under the kitchen sink.

B: Oh, good. I (be) _____ happy to get that pipe fixed.

PRACTICE 12 ▶ Using the present progressive and the simple present to express future time. (Chart 3-4)

Complete the second sentence with a form of the present progressive to express the same meaning as the first sentence.

1. I'm going to see the dentist tomorrow. I _____*'m seeing*_____ the dentist tomorrow.

2. Jada will have her baby in July. She _____ her baby in July.

3. The new store will open in September. It _____ in September.

4. Most employees are going to work late tonight. They _____ late tonight.

5. We're going to have a graduation party for Miriam on Saturday. We _____ a graduation party for Miriam on Saturday.

6. Shelley and Sue are going to attend the conference in New York next April. They _____ the conference in New York next April.

PRACTICE 13 ▶ Using the present progressive and the simple present to express future time. (Chart 3-4)

Choose all the possible completions for each sentence.

1. We have tickets for a concert today. It _____ at 7:00 P.M.
   a. starts
   b. is starting
   c. is going to start

2. Look at those black clouds! Pretty soon it _____.
   a. rains
   b. is raining
   c. is going to rain

3. This afternoon I'm having lunch with a friend. After that, we _____ her aunt.
   a. are going to visit
   b. are visiting
   c. visit

4. I'm hurrying to catch a plane. It _____ in an hour!
   a. leaves
   b. is going to leave
   c. is leaving

5. Sorry I can't meet with you tomorrow, Helen. I have an important appointment. I _____ with the president at noon.
   a. 'm meeting
   b. 'm going to meet
   c. will meet

6. A: Nobody has volunteered to bring the drinks for the festival Saturday night. Olga, how about you? Harry, how about you? Please ... can somebody help us out?

   B: OK, OK. I _____ it.
   a. 'll do
   b. 'm doing
   c. 'm going to do

PRACTICE 14 ▶ Using the present progressive to express future time. (Chart 3-4)
Change the verbs in *italics* to a form of the present progressive for a planned event or definite intention. If no change is possible, write "NC."

1. A: The package needs to be there tomorrow. Will it get there in time?

   B: Don't worry. *I'm going to send* it by express mail.

        I'm sending it by express mail.

2. A: What's the weather report?

   B: *It is going to rain* tomorrow morning.

        NC

3. A: Would you like to have dinner with me tonight, Pat?

   B: Thanks, but *I'm going to have* dinner with my sister and her husband.

        _____

4. A: What *are you going to do* this evening?

        _____

   B: *I'm going to study* at the library.

        _____

5. A: Oh, I spilled my coffee on the floor.

   B: *I'll help* you clean it up.

        _____

6. A: Did you know that Kathy and Paul are engaged?

   B: No. That's great! When *are they going to get* married?

   A: In September.

   _____

7. A: *You're going to laugh* when I tell you what happened to me today!

   B: Oh? What happened?

   _____

8. A: Have you lived here long?

   B: No, not long. Only about a year. But *we're going to move* again next month. My father's company has reassigned him to Atlanta, Georgia.

   _____

9. A: I tried to register for Professor Stein's economics class, but it's full. *Is he going to teach* it again next semester?

   B: I think so.

   _____

10. A: Son, *I'm not going to send* you any money this month. You're spending far too much. You need to learn to be more careful.

   _____

   B: But Dad ... !

   A: Just do the best you can. *I am going to visit* you next month. We can talk about it then.

   _____

PRACTICE 15 ▸ Future progressive. (Chart 3-5)
Complete the sentences. Write the future progressive form of the verbs in blue.

1. Every night at 7:00 I read a book. Tomorrow at 7:10, I

   _____ a book.

2. We fly to Italy tomorrow night. Tomorrow night at this time, we

   _____ over the Atlantic Ocean.

3. On Sunday mornings, I sleep late. Next Sunday morning at 9:00 A.M., I

   _____ .

4. It always snows in December in Moscow. We're going to Moscow in December. At that time, it

   _____ in Moscow.

5. Ellen always watches late movies on TV. I'm sure that tonight she

   _____ an old movie on TV around 2:00 A.M.

PRACTICE 16 ▸ Future progressive. (Charts 3-3 and 3-5)
Complete the sentences with the future progressive or the simple present form of the verbs in parentheses.

1. Just relax, Antoine. As soon as your sprained ankle (*heal*) _____*heals*_____, you can play soccer

   again. At this time next week, you (*play*) _____*will be playing*_____ soccer again.

2. I'll meet you at the airport tomorrow. After you (*go*) _____ customs, look for me just

   outside the gate. I (*stand*) _____ right by the door.

3. Ingrid and Ruth won't be at this school when classes (*start*) _____ next semester.

   They (*attend*) _____ a new school in Taiwan.

4. Please come and visit today when you (*have*) _____ a chance. I

   (*shop*) _____ from 1:00 to about 3:00, but I'll be home after that.

5. I won't be here next week, students. I (*attend*) _____ a seminar out

   of town. Ms. Gomez will be the substitute teacher. When I (*return*) _____, I will

   expect you to be ready for the midterm examination.

PRACTICE 17 ▶ Future perfect and future perfect progressive. (Chart 3-6)
Complete the sentences with the future perfect or the future perfect progressive form of the verbs in the box. Include any words in parentheses. Use each verb only once.

drink	fly	land	listen	ride	✓ rise	save	teach

1. By the time I get up tomorrow morning, the sun (*already*) ___*will already have risen*___.

2. This is a long trip! By the time we get to Miami, we _____ on

   this bus for over 15 hours.

3. We're going to be late. By the time we get to the airport, my brother's plane

   (*already*) _____.

4. He's never going to stop talking. In 15 more minutes, we _____

   to him lecture for three solid hours. I don't even know what he's saying anymore.

5. I drink too much coffee. I have already had two cups this morning, and I will probably have

   two more cups. This means that before lunch, I _____ four

   cups of coffee.

6. This is the longest flight I have ever taken. By the time we get to New Zealand, we

   _____ for 13 hours. I'm going to be exhausted.

7. Douglas has been putting some money away every month to prepare for his trip to South America

   next year. By the end of this year, he _____ enough.

8. Can you believe it? According to our grammar teacher, by the end of this semester, she

   _____ more than 3,000 students from 42 different countries.

   She has been teaching for nearly 20 years — and she still loves it!

PRACTICE 18 ▶ Chapter review.
These sentences describe typical events in a day in the life of a woman named Kathy. The sentences are in the past, but all of these things will happen in Kathy's life tomorrow. Change all of the sentences to the future. Use **will**.

1. When Kathy got up yesterday morning, the sun was shining. The same thing will happen

   tomorrow. When Kathy ___*gets*___ up tomorrow morning, the sun

   ___*will be shining*___.

2. Yesterday she brushed her teeth and showered. Then she made a light breakfast. Tomorrow will be the same. She _____ her teeth and _____. Then she _____ a light breakfast.

3. After she ate breakfast yesterday, she got ready to go to work. And tomorrow after she _____ breakfast, she _____ ready to go to work.

4. By the time she got to work yesterday, she had drunk three cups of coffee. Tomorrow she'll do the same. By the time she _____ to work, she _____ three cups of coffee.

5. Between 8:00 and 9:00, Kathy answered her email and planned her day. She has the same plans for tomorrow. Between 8:00 and 9:00, Kathy _____ her email and _____ her day.

6. By 10:00 yesterday, she had called three new clients. Tomorrow, by 10:00, she _____ three new clients.

7. At 11:00 yesterday, she was attending a staff meeting. She plans to do the same tomorrow. At 11:00, she _____ a staff meeting.

8. She went to lunch at noon and had a sandwich and a bowl of soup. Tomorrow she _____ to lunch at noon and _____ a sandwich and a bowl of soup.

9. After she finished eating, she took a short walk in the park before she returned to the office. Tomorrow she'll do the same. After she _____ eating, she _____ a walk in the park before she _____ to the office.

10. She worked at her desk until she went to another meeting in the middle of the afternoon. And tomorrow she _____ at her desk until she _____ to another meeting in the middle of the afternoon.

11. By the time she left the office, she had attended three meetings. Tomorrow she'll follow the same schedule. By the time she _____ the office, she _____ three meetings.

12. When Kathy got home, her children were playing in the yard, and Grandma was watching them from the porch. Tomorrow will be the same. When Kathy _____ home, her children _____ in the yard, and Grandma _____ them from the porch.

13. The children had been playing since 3:00 in the afternoon. And tomorrow they _____ since 3:00 in the afternoon.

14. The family had dinner together and talked about their day. Tomorrow will be the same. They _____ dinner together, and they _____ about their day.

15. They watched television for a while, and then Kathy and her husband put the kids to bed. The same thing will happen tomorrow. They _____ television for a while, and then they _____ the kids to bed.

16. By the time Kathy went to bed yesterday, she had had a full day and was ready for sleep.

Tomorrow will be the same for Kathy. By the time she _____ to bed, she

_____ a full day and _____ ready for sleep.

PRACTICE 19 ▸ Chapter review.
There is one verb error in each sentence. Correct the error.

1. Next month, I'm travel to Europe with my sister.

2. My sister is going to attends an academic conference in Amsterdam.

3. While she is attending the conference, I'll touring the city.

4. After Amsterdam, we are going go to Ibiza.

5. When I'll be there, I'm going to swim in the Mediterranean.

6. My sister and I are going to visit a few other cities in Spain before we'll go to Lisbon.

7. By the end of our trip, we'll have been travel for two weeks.

8. When I return home, I'll have visit three European countries.

9. It's going be an awesome vacation.

Review of Verb Tenses

PRACTICE 1 ▸ Verb tense review. (Chapters 1 → 3)
Read the passage. <u>Underline</u> the 16 verbs.

Cooking Class

Central Market is offering two classes this month. If you are curious about Indian Food, then Tandoori Nights is the class for you. This class will meet every Friday night 6:00–8:00. Instructor Elaine Adams had owned a small café in India for several years before she returned to the United States last year. She is going to focus primarily on chicken and vegetarian dishes from northern India. For Spanish food enthusiasts, we are offering Spanish Style Slow Cooking. This class meets Saturday afternoons 2:00–4:00. Instructor Ruben Reyes has been teaching classes at Central Market for nearly

twenty years. He has written three cookbooks on Spanish and Mediterranean cuisine. His newest book explores the art of slow cooking. His class introduces students to several main dishes. If you haven't registered, there is still time, but classes are getting full.

---

1. Write the six verbs in the simple present tense.

   _____

2. Write the two verbs in the present progressive tense.

   _____

3. Write the verb in the simple past tense.

   _____

4. Write the two verbs in the simple future tense.

   _____

5. Write the two verbs in the present perfect tense.

   _____

6. Write the verb in the present perfect progressive tense.

   _____

7. Write the verb in the past perfect tense.

   _____

PRACTICE 2 ▸ Verb tense review. (Chapters 1 → 3)

Complete the sentences with the correct form of the verbs in parentheses.

1. A: I'm going to ask you some questions so that we can practice verb tenses. What do you do every day before you come to class? Name one thing.

   B: I (eat) _____ *eat* _____ breakfast.

2. A: What did you do last night? Name three separate activities.

   B: Last night I (eat) _____ dinner. Then I (visit) _____ some friends, and later I (write) _____ a couple of letters.

3. A: What are you doing right now? What activity is in progress right now, at this exact moment?

   B: Right now I (talk) _____ to you. I (answer) _____ your questions.

4. A: Think about this exact time yesterday. What activity was in progress then?

   B: Let me see. At this time yesterday, I was at the library. I (study) _____ for a test.

5. A: How many questions have I asked since we began this exercise?

   B: I think you (ask) _____ me five or six questions since we began this exercise.

6. A: What have you been doing for the past five minutes? In other words, what activity began five minutes ago and has been in progress from then until now?

   B: I (talk) _____ to you for the past five minutes. I started talking to you five minutes ago, and I am still talking to you.

7. A: Where will you be tomorrow morning?

   B: I (be) _____ in class tomorrow morning.

8. A: What will you be doing at this exact time tomorrow? In other words, what activity will be in progress at this exact same time tomorrow?

   B: Right now I am sitting in the classroom. And at this exact time tomorrow, I (sit) _____ in the classroom.

PRACTICE 3 ▸ Verb tense review. (Chapters 1 → 3)

Choose the correct completions.

1. My grandfather   has never flown / had never flown   in an airplane, and he has no plans to ever fly.

2. Jane isn't here yet. I   am waiting / have been waiting   for her since noon, but she still didn't arrive / hasn't arrived.

3. In all the world, there   have been / are   only 14 mountains that   reach / are reaching   above 8,000 meters (26,247 feet).

4. When my parents were teenagers, people   hadn't owned / didn't own   computers. By the time I was a teenager, I   was owning / had owned   a computer for several years.

5. Right now we   are having / have   a heat wave. The temperature   is / has been   in the upper 90s Fahrenheit (30s Celsius) for the last six days.

6. I have a long trip ahead of me tomorrow, so I think I'd better go to bed. Let me say good-bye now because I won't see you in the morning. I   will leave / will have left   by the time you get / will get   up.

7. Last night I   went / was going   to a party. When I   get / got   there, the room was full of people. Some of them   danced / were dancing   and others   talked / were talking.   One young woman   was standing / has been standing   by herself. I   have never met / had never met   her before, so I   introduced / was introducing   myself to her.

8. About three o'clock yesterday afternoon, Jessica   was sitting / had sat   in bed reading a book. Suddenly, she   heard / was hearing   a loud noise and   got / was getting   up to see what it was. She   has looked / looked   out the window. A truck   has just backed / had just backed   into her new car!

PRACTICE 4 ▶ Verb tense review. (Chapters 1 → 3)
Choose the correct completions.

1. Next month I have a week's vacation. I   take / am taking   a trip. I   leave / left   on Saturday, July 2nd. First, I   've gone / 'm going   to Madison, Wisconsin, to visit my brother. After I   will leave / leave   Madison, I   am going to go / have gone   to Chicago to see a friend who is studying / will have studied   at the university there. She   has lived / lives   in Chicago for three years, so she   knows / knew   her way around the city. She   has promised / will be promising   to take me to many interesting places. I   had never been / have never been   to Chicago, so I am looking / have looked   forward to going there.

2. The weather is beautiful today, but until this morning, it   has been raining / had been raining   steadily for almost a week. A week ago, the temperature suddenly   was dropping / dropped,   and after that we had bad weather for a week. Now the weather forecaster says that tomorrow it is going to be / is   very warm. The weather certainly   was changing / changes   quickly here. I never know what to expect. Who knows? When I   wake / will wake   up tomorrow morning, maybe it   snows / will be snowing.

PRACTICE 5 ▶ Verb tense review. (Chapters 1 → 3)
Complete the sentences with the verbs in parentheses. Use any appropriate tense.

On June 20th, I returned home. I (be) _____ away from home for two years. My
                                                        1
family (meet) _____ me at the airport with kisses and tears. They (miss) _____ me
                    2   3
as much as I had missed them. I (be) _____ very happy to see them again.
                                                    4

When I (get) _____ the chance, I (take) _____ a long look at them. My
                        5   6
little brother (be) _____ no longer little. He (grow) _____ a lot. He
                                7   8
(be) _____ almost as tall as my father. My little sister (wear) _____
            9   10
a green dress. She (change) _____ quite a bit too, but she
                                        11
(be, still) _____ very curious. She (ask) _____ me a thousand
                    12   13
questions a minute, or so it seemed.

My father (*gain*) _____ 14 _____ some weight, and his hair
(*turn*) _____ 15 _____ a little grayer, but otherwise he was just as I had remembered him.
My mother (*look*) _____ 16 _____ a little older, but not much. The wrinkles on her
face (*be*) _____ 17 _____ smile wrinkles.

PRACTICE 6 ▶ Verb tense review. (Chapters 1 → 3)
Complete the sentences with the verbs in the box. Use any appropriate tense.

be	break	do	happen	have	play	recuperate	see

A: Where's Sonia? I (*not*) _____ 1 _____ her lately.

B: She _____ 2 _____ at home from an accident.

A: An accident? What _____ 3 _____ to her?

B: She _____ 4 _____ her arm while she _____ 5 _____ volleyball last week in the
game against South City College.

A: Gosh, that's too bad. I'm sorry to hear that. How _____ 6 _____ she _____ 7 _____ ?

B: OK, I guess. Actually, she _____ 8 _____ a cast on her arm, but she is not in any pain. I
think that she _____ 9 _____ back in class next week.

PRACTICE 7 ▶ Verb tense review. (Chapters 1 → 3)
Complete the sentences with the verbs in parentheses. Use any appropriate tense.

A: Have you ever heard of the Socratic method?

B: No, I haven't. What is it?

A: It's a method of teaching that Socrates (*use*) _____ 1 _____ in ancient Greece more
than two thousand years ago. Some teachers still (*use*) _____ 2 _____ this kind of
method today.

B: Really? What (*it, consist*) _____ 3 _____ of today? How
(*teachers, use*) _____ 4 _____ this method now?

A: Well, the teacher (*not, give*) _____ 5 _____ any information to the students. She
or he just asks a series of questions, but (*not, make*) _____ 6 _____ any statements.
The teacher (*know*) _____ 7 _____ what the important questions to ask the students are.
Then the students have to think about the answers.

B: That (*sound*) _____ 8 _____ good to me! When I was in high school, I had a lot of
teachers who just (*talk*) _____ 9 _____ too much. Sometimes the students even
(*fall*) _____ 10 _____ asleep in class!

A: I (*agree*) _____ 11 _____ with you. You will learn faster after you
(*think*) _____ 12 _____ about something than if you just have to remember facts.

B: That's true. I (*take*) _____ a philosophy class now with a wonderful

13

professor. She (*always, ask*) _____ questions! I guess she

14

(*use*) _____ the Socratic method for the whole semester, and I

15

(*not, realize*) _____ it!

16

PRACTICE 8 ▸ Verb tense review. (Chapters 1 → 3)
Complete the sentences with the correct form of the verbs in parentheses.

1. Nora is at the hospital because her cousin is having surgery today. The surgery began at 7:00 and is expected to end at noon. Nora arrived at the hospital at 8:00 A.M.

   a. It's 8:10 A.M. Nora (*wait*) _____ in the waiting room.

   b. It is now 9:00 A.M. Nora (*wait*) _____ for one hour.

   c. By 11:00, the surgery will still be going on, and Nora will still be waiting in the waiting room. At that time, Nora (*wait*) _____ in the waiting room for three hours.

2. Hundreds of passengers are in the security line at the airport. Jaime entered the security line at 8:00 A.M.

   a. It's 8:15 A.M. Jaime (*stand*) _____ in the security line at the airport.

   b. It is now 9:00 A.M. Jaime (*stand*) _____ in the security line for an hour.

   c. Jaime is probably going to be standing in the security line for another hour. By 9:30 A.M., he (*stand*) _____ in the security line for an hour and a half.

   d. Jaime is probably going to be finished standing in the security line by 10:00 A.M. If he is finished at 10:00 A.M., he (*stand*) _____ in line for a total of two hours!

PRACTICE 9 ▸ Verb tense review. (Chapters 1 → 3)
Choose the correct completions.

1. A: Hurry up! We're waiting for you. What's taking you so long?

   B: I _____ for an important phone call. Go ahead and leave without me.
      a. wait   c. have waited
      b. will have waited   d. am waiting

2. A: Robert is going to be famous someday. He _____ in three movies already.

   B: I'm sure he'll be a star.
      a. has been appearing   c. has appeared
      b. had appeared   d. appeared

3. A: Where's Polly?

   B: She _____.
      a. is in her room studying   c. studies in her room
      b. in her room is studying   d. has studied in her room

4. A: What _____ of the new simplified tax law?

   B: It's more confusing than the old one.
      a. are you thinking   c. have you thought
      b. do you think   d. have you been thinking

5. A: When is Mr. Fields planning to retire?

   B: Soon, I think. He _____ here for a long time. He'll probably retire either next year or the year
      after that.
      a. worked   c. has been working
      b. had been working   d. is working

6. A: Why did you buy all this sugar and chocolate?

   B: I _____ a delicious chocolate cake for dinner tonight.
      a. make   c. 'm going to make
      b. will make   d. will have made

7. A: Let's go! What's taking you so long?

   B: I'll be there as soon as I _____ my keys.
      a. find   c. 'm going to find
      b. will find   d. am finding

8. Next week when there _____ a full moon, the ocean tides will be higher.
      a. is being   c. is
      b. will be   d. will have been

9. While I _____ TV last night, a mouse ran across the floor.
      a. have watched   c. watched
      b. was watching   d. have been watching

10. Fish were among the earliest forms of life. Fish _____ on earth for ages and ages.
      a. existed   c. exist
      b. are existing   d. have existed

11. The phone _____ constantly since Jack announced his candidacy for president this morning.
      a. has been ringing   c. had rung
      b. rang   d. had been ringing

12. The earth _____ on the sun for its heat and light.
      a. depended   c. was depending
      b. depending   d. depends

13. I don't feel good. I _____ home from work tomorrow.
      a. 'm staying   c. stay
      b. will have stayed   d. stayed

14. Today there are weather satellites that send down information about the earth's atmosphere. In the
    last several decades, space exploration _____ great contributions to weather forecasting.
      a. is making   c. makes
      b. has made   d. made

15. On July 20th, 1969, astronaut Neil Armstrong _____ down onto the moon. He was the first person
    ever to set foot on another celestial body.
      a. was stepping   c. stepped
      b. has stepped   d. has been stepping

16. Mechanical problems delayed the flight. When the tired passengers finally boarded the aircraft,
    many were annoyed and irritable because they _____ in the airport for three and a half hours.
      a. are waiting   c. have been waiting
      b. were waiting   d. had been waiting

17. If rising sea levels continue at the present rate, in another 50 years this town _____ anymore.
      a. doesn't exist   c. isn't existing
      b. isn't going to exist   d. won't be existing

18. Homestead High School's football team _____ a championship until last season when the new coach led them to win first place in their league.
    a. has never won
    b. is never winning
    c. had never been winning
    d. had never won

19. Nonnative speakers need many years of intensive language study before they can qualify as interpreters. By the end of this year, Chen _____ English for three years, but he will still need more training and experience before he masters the language.
    a. will be studying
    b. has studied
    c. will have been studying
    d. has been studying

PRACTICE 10 ▶ Verb tense review. (Chapters 1 → 3)
Choose the correct completions.

1. A: May I speak to Dr. Paine, please?

   B: I'm sorry, he _____ a patient at the moment. Can I help you?
      a. is seeing
      b. sees
      c. was seeing
      d. has been seeing

2. A: When are you going to ask your boss for a raise?

   B: I _____ to her twice already! I don't think she wants to give me one.
      a. 've talked
      b. was talking
      c. 've been talking
      d. 'd talked

3. A: Do you think Harry will want something to eat after he gets here?

   B: I hope not. It'll probably be after midnight, and we _____.
      a. are sleeping
      b. will be sleeping
      c. have been sleeping
      d. be sleeping

4. Paul, could you please turn off the stove? The potatoes _____ for at least 30 minutes.
      a. are boiling
      b. boiling
      c. have been boiling
      d. were boiling

5. A: I once saw a turtle that had wings. The turtle flew into the air to catch insects.

   B: Stop kidding. I _____ you!
      a. don't believe
      b. am not believing
      c. didn't believe
      d. wasn't believing

6. A: Is it true that spaghetti didn't originate in Italy?

   B: Yes. The Chinese _____ spaghetti dishes for a long time before Marco Polo brought it back to Italy.
      a. have been making
      b. have made
      c. had been making
      d. make

7. A: Could someone help me lift the lawnmower into the pickup truck?

   B: I'm not busy. I _____ you.
      a. help
      b. 'll help
      c. am helping
      d. am going to help

8. My family loves this house. It _____ the family home ever since my grandfather built it 60 years ago.
      a. was
      b. has been
      c. will be
      d. is

9. Here's an interesting statistic: On a typical day, the average person _____ about 48,000 words. How many words did you use today?
   a. used
   b. was using
   c. is using
   d. uses

10. It's against the law to kill the black rhinoceros. They _____ extinct.
    a. became
    b. have become
    c. are becoming
    d. become

11. After ten unhappy years, Janice finally quit her job. She _____ along with her boss for a long time before she finally decided to look for a new position.
    a. hadn't been getting
    b. isn't getting
    c. didn't get
    d. hasn't been getting

12. The National Hurricane Center is closely watching a strong hurricane over the Atlantic Ocean. When it _____ the coast of Texas sometime tomorrow afternoon, it will bring with it great destructive force.
    a. reaches
    b. will reach
    c. reaching
    d. is reaching

13. At one time, huge prehistoric reptiles dominated the earth. This Age of Dinosaurs _____ much longer than the present Age of Mammals has lasted to date.
    a. lasted
    b. was lasting
    c. had lasted
    d. has lasted

14. Jim, why don't you take some time off? You _____ too hard lately. Take a short vacation.
    a. worked
    b. work
    c. have been working
    d. were working

15. The city is rebuilding its run-down waterfront, transforming it into a pleasant and fashionable outdoor mall. Next summer when the tourists arrive, they _____ 104 beautiful new shops and restaurants.
    a. will found
    b. will be finding
    c. will find
    d. will have found

16. A minor earthquake occurred at 2:07 A.M. on January 3rd. Most of the people in the village _____ at the time and didn't even know it had occurred until the next morning.
    a. slept
    b. had slept
    c. sleep
    d. were sleeping

17. The little girl started to cry. She _____ her doll, and no one was able to find it for her.
    a. has lost
    b. had lost
    c. was lost
    d. was losing

18. According to research, people usually _____ in their sleep 25 to 30 times each night.
    a. turn
    b. are turning
    c. turned
    d. have turned

CHAPTER 5

Subject-Verb Agreement

PRACTICE 1 ▸ Preview.
Read the passage. Choose the correct completions.

> ### 10,000 Hours
>
> The key to success   is / are   a lot of practice and hard work. Malcolm Gladwell, in his book *Outliers*,   explain / explains   the 10,000-hour rule. According to Gladwell, 10,000 hours of practice   is / are   enough to become an expert in almost any field. That's about three hours every single day for ten straight years. Gladwell   provides / provide   several examples.
>
>
>
> The Beatles   was / were   one of the most successful musical groups in history. Before the Beatles became famous, the band members played near military bases in Germany for eight hours a day, seven days a week. They did this for a year and a half. They had performed about 1,200 times before they reached commercial success. That   is / are   more than most bands today perform in their entire career.
>
> Another example   is / are   Bill Gates. Most people   agrees / agree   Gates is a computer genius. When Gates   was / were   in school in the 1960s, computer programming was not very popular. Most schools didn't have computer classes or clubs, but Gates   was / were   lucky. He attended a school that had advanced technology. He began programming in the eighth grade. By the time he finished high school, he had already completed several hundred hours of computer programming.
>
> Is / Are   there a skill you have practiced for 10,000 hours? What do you think?   Is / Are   10,000 hours enough to make you an expert?

PRACTICE 2 ▸ Final -s on nouns and verbs. (Chart 5-1)
Look at the words that end in **-s**. Check (✓) the correct columns.

	Noun	Verb	Singular	Plural
1. a. A boat floats.		✓	✓	
b. Boats float.				
2. a. My friend lives in my neighborhood.				
b. My friends live in my neighborhood.				
3. a. Helen eats a donut every morning.				
b. Donuts contain a lot of sugar.				
4. a. Babies cry when they are hungry.				
b. My baby cries every night.				

PRACTICE 3 ▸ Spelling of final -s / -es. (Chart 5-1)
Complete the sentences with **-s** or **-es**.

1. Holly teach _es_ English at a community college.

2. Her class_____ are from 9:00 A.M. till 1:00 P.M. five day_____ a week.

3. She use_____ a lot of song_____ and game_____ in her lesson_____.

4. When she finish_____ work at the college each day, she go_____ to the gym.

5. After she exercise_____, she pick_____ her children up from school.

PRACTICE 4 ▸ Basic subject-verb agreement. (Chart 5-2)
Choose the correct completions.

1. The weather   is / are   cold.

2. Vegetables   is / are   good for you.

3. Each student   has / have   a locker in the gym.

4. A dog   barks / bark.

5. Dogs   barks / bark.

6. Ann   is / are   at home.

7. Ann and Sue   is / are   at home.

8. Every student and teacher   is / are   here today.

9. A student and teacher   is / are   talking in the hallway.

10. Eating vegetables   is / are   good for you.

PRACTICE 5 ▸ Collective nouns. (Chart 5-3)
Complete the sentences with **is** or **are**. Use **is** when possible.

1. a. The faculty _____ forming a new committee.

   b. The committee _____ meeting next month.

   c. Committee members _____ responsible for new policy decisions.

2. a. Our college basketball team _____ the best in the league.

   b. The team members _____ on the cover of a sports magazine this month.

   c. Tonight is the final game of the season. The crowd _____ very excited.

3. a. The school choir _____ performing three concerts this weekend.

   b. Choir members _____ rehearsing today.

PRACTICE 6 ▸ Collective nouns. (Chart 5-3)
Decide if the word in blue refers to a unit or emphasizes the individual members.

1. The team practices five nights a week.	a unit	the individual members
2. The public is still unaware of the situation.	a unit	the individual members
3. The staff are available from 9:00 to 5:00.	a unit	the individual members
4. The family has a reunion every year.	a unit	the individual members
5. The faculty have a semester break this week.	a unit	the individual members
6. The government is passing a new law.	a unit	the individual members

PRACTICE 7 ▸ Subject-verb agreement: using expressions of quantity. (Chart 5-4)
Complete the sentences with *is* or *are*.

1. a. Some of Highway 21 _____ closed due to flooding.

   b. Some of the highways _____ closed due to flooding.

2. a. A lot of that movie _____ full of violence.

   b. A lot of movies _____ full of violence.

3. a. Half of the pizza _____ for you and half _____ for me.

   b. Half of the pizzas _____ vegetarian.

4. a. Most of my friends _____ people I met in school.

   b. Every one of my friends _____ a sports fan.

5. a. The number of desks in that classroom _____ 35.

   b. A number of stores _____ closed today because of the holiday.

PRACTICE 8 ▸ Subject-verb agreement: using expressions of quantity. (Chart 5-4)
Choose the correct completions.

1. A large part of our town   have / has   been badly damaged by a big fire.
2. Most of the houses   was / were   destroyed by the fire.
3. Most of the house   was / were   destroyed by the fire.
4. One of the houses   was / were   destroyed by the fire.
5. Each of the houses   is / are   in ruins.
6. Each house   is / are   in ruins.
7. Every one of the houses   has / have   serious damage.
8. Every house   has / have   serious damage.
9. None of the houses   has / have   escaped damage.

PRACTICE 9 ▸ Subject-verb agreement: using *there + be*. (Chart 5-5)
Choose the correct completions.

1. There   is / are   a cup on the table.
2. There   is / are   some cups on the table.
3. There   is / are   a lot of people in the line for the movie.
4. There   is / are   a snack bar in the lobby of the theater.
5. There   wasn't / weren't   any hurricanes in Florida last year.
6. There   was / were   a terrible tsunami in Asia in 2004.
7. Why   isn't / aren't   there any windows in the classroom?
8. Why   isn't / aren't   there a teacher in the classroom?
9. There   has / have   been an ongoing problem with the color printer.
10. There   has / have   been a lot of problems with the color printer.

PRACTICE 10 ▸ Subject-verb agreement: some irregularities. (Chart 5-6)
Choose the correct completions.

1. States   is / are   political units.

2. The United States   is / are   in North America.

3. The news in that newspaper   is / are   biased.

4. Economics   is / are   an important area of study.

5. Diabetes   is / are   an illness. Mumps   is / are   another kind of illness. Rabies   is / are   a disease you can get from an infected animal.

6. One hundred meters   isn't / aren't   a long distance to travel by car.

7. Five minutes   isn't / aren't   too long to wait.

8. Six and four   is / are   ten.

9. People   is / are   interesting.

10. English   is / are   a common language.

11. The English   is / are   friendly people.

12. The elderly in my country   is / are   given free medical care.

13. Four colorful fish   is / are   swimming in the fish tank.

14. The police   is / are   coming to investigate the accident.

PRACTICE 11 ▸ Subject-verb agreement. (Charts 5-2 → 5-6)
Complete the sentences with the present tense of the appropriate verb in the box. Some verbs may be used more than once.

be	contain	cost	drive	like	make	remind

1. There _____ an old barn near our town. The barn has been converted to a

   bookstore, and its name is The Old Barn Bookstore.

2. It's a very popular place, especially on weekends. People _____ it a lot. They

   _____ out to the barn on weekends.

3. It's about twenty miles from downtown. Twenty miles _____ a long drive, but the bookstore is worth the drive.

4. A lot of the books in The Old Barn Bookstore _____ not new books. There _____ a lot of used books, old books, and even valuable antique books.

5. There _____ a large number of beautiful art books too. Each one _____ excellent photographs of famous pieces of art. Most of these books _____ quite expensive.

6. One of the books _____ over a hundred dollars because it is very valuable. It has an autograph and an inscription by Ernest Hemingway.

7. There _____ a small café in The Old Barn Bookstore too. The number of food items on the menu _____ very small, but about twenty different kinds of coffee _____ served.

8. Last Sunday I was browsing through some books when I heard a group of people speaking French. I used to understand French, but now French _____ very difficult for me to understand. However, hearing French always _____ me of my days as a student and _____ me feel young again.

PRACTICE 12 ▸ Subject-verb agreement. (Charts 5-2 → 5-6)
Choose the correct completions.

1. Each skater in the competition   has / have   trained since childhood.

2. A convention of English teachers from all over the world   take / takes   place every spring.

3. Some of the new movies   is / are   good, but a lot of them   has / have   too much violence.

4. We saw a film about India last night. Some of the movie   was / were   fascinating, and there   was / were   a lot of beautiful mountain scenes.

5. Three-fourths of the patients who   take / takes   this new medicine report improvement.

6. Almost three-quarters of the surface of the earth   is / are   covered by water.

7. There   is / are   100 senators in the United States Senate. The number of votes necessary for a simple majority   is / are   51.

8. There   has / have   been some encouraging news about pandas in recent years. There   is / are   more pandas living today than there   was / were   ten years ago.

9. The United Arab Emirates   is / are   a country in the Middle East.

10. The *New York Times*   is / are   an important newspaper.

11. Economics   is / are   impossible for me to understand.

12. Diabetes   is / are   an illness. People who   has / have   it must be careful with their diet.

13. Five dollars   is / are   too much to pay for a pencil!

14. The English   speak / speaks   with an accent that is different from the American accent.

15. The handicapped   use / uses   a special entrance in this building.

PRACTICE 13 ▶ Subject-verb agreement. (Chapters 1–5)
Complete the sentences with the correct form of the verbs in parentheses. Use any appropriate tense.

1. Nearly 90% of the people in our town always (*vote*) _____ in local elections.

2. In recent years, a number of students (*participate*) _____ in language programs abroad.

3. The number of students who knew the answer to the last question on the exam (*be*) _____ very low.

4. Every one of the boys and girls in the school (*know*) _____ what to do if the fire alarm rings.

5. A lot of people in the United States (*speak*) _____ and (*understand*) _____ Spanish.

6. Why (*be*) _____ the police standing over there right now?

7. Why (*broadcast*) _____ most of the television stations _____ news at the same hour every night?

8. Some of the most important books for my report (*be*) _____ not available in the school library, so I'll have to look for information on the Internet.

9. Recently there (*be*) _____ times when I have seriously considered dropping out of school.

10. Not one of the women in my office (*receive*) _____ a promotion in the past two years. All of the promotions (*go*) _____ to men.

11. The news on the radio and TV stations (*confirm*) _____ that a serious storm is approaching our city.

12. Geography (*be*) _____ fascinating. Mathematics (*be*) _____ fascinating. I love those subjects!

13. Mathematics and geography (*be*) _____ my favorite subjects.

14. By law, every man, woman, and child (*have*) _____ the right to free speech. It is guaranteed in our constitution.

15. (*Be, not*) _____ sugar and pineapple the leading crops in Hawaii now?

16. Why (*be*) _____ there a shortage of qualified school teachers at the present time?

17. How many states in the United States (*begin*) _____ with the letter "A"?*

18. The United States (*consist*) _____ of 50 states.

19. What places in the world (*have*) _____ no snakes?

20. Politics (*be*) _____ a constant source of interest to me.

21. (*Be*) _____ there ever any doubt in your mind about the outcome of the election? You were sure that Garcia was going to win, weren't you?

---

*See the Answer Key for the answer to this question.

Correct the errors in the use of singular and plural forms of nouns and verbs. Do not add any new words.

1. My mother wear~s~∧ glasses.

2. Elephants is large animals.

3. Your heart beat faster when you exercise.

4. Healthy hearts needs regular exercise.

5. Every child in the class know the alphabet.

6. Some of the magazine at the dentist's office are two year old.

7. A number of the students in my class is from Mexico.

8. One of my favorite subject in school is algebra.

9. There's many different kind of insects in the world.

10. Writing compositions are difficult for me.

11. The United States have a population of over 300 million.

12. Most of the movie take place in Paris.

13. Most of the people in my factory division likes and gets along with one another, but a few of the worker doesn't fit in with the rest of us very well.

CHAPTER 6

Nouns

PRACTICE 1 ▶ Preview.
Read the passage. Answer the questions.

The Green Exchange Program

The "Green Exchange Program" in Curitiba, Brazil allows people to exchange <u>household</u> trash for food. Residents of the city take cardboard, glass, metal, and paper to a recycling center. In exchange, they get fresh food, such as fruit, vegetables, and eggs. People can also exchange their trash for <u>bus</u> tickets. <u>Curitiba's</u> recycling program is very effective. Ninety percent of its residents recycle about two-thirds of their trash every day.

---

1. Which word in blue is a singular count noun?

   _____

2. Which three words in blue are plural count nouns?

   _____

3. Which five words in blue are noncount nouns?

   _____

4. Which <u>underlined</u> word shows possession?

   _____

5. Which two <u>underlined</u> words are nouns used as adjectives?

   _____

PRACTICE 2 ▶ Regular and irregular plural nouns. (Chart 6-1)
Write the plural forms of the given nouns.

1. one car, two _____
2. one woman, two _____
3. one match, two _____
4. one mouse, two _____
5. one city, two _____
6. one donkey, two _____
7. one half, two _____
8. one chief, two _____

9. one class, two _____
10. one foot, two _____
11. one hero, two _____
12. one piano, two _____
13. one video, two _____
14. one basis, two _____
15. one bacterium, two _____
16. one series, two _____

PRACTICE 3 ▸ Regular and irregular plural nouns. (Chart 6-1)

Complete the sentences with the correct plural form of the nouns in the box. Use each word once.

belief	fish	monkey	species	thief
child	kilo	✓ potato	stereo	tooth

1. I had my favorite vegetable for dinner: delicious fried _____potatoes_____.

2. At the zoo, we saw a lot of _____ jumping around in the trees.

3. The police caught the two _____ who had stolen over 100 _____
   from people's cars.

4. The shopping mall has a playground for _____.

5. Our baby got two new _____ this week!

6. The two families found that they hold the same _____; they believe in the
   same things.

7. Some people think that whales are a species of _____, but they are not; they are
   mammals.

8. The adult male of some _____ of bears weighs about 600 _____.

PRACTICE 4 ▸ Final -s / -es. (Chart 6-1)

Add final **-s** / **-es** where necessary. Do not change, add, or omit any other words in the sentences.

1. A bird care͢ˢ for its feather͢ˢ by cleaning them with its beak.

2. There are many occupation in the world. Doctor take care of sick people. Pilot fly airplane.
   Professor teach class. Farmer raise crop.

3. An architect design building. An archeologist dig in the ground to find object from past
   civilizations.

4. The first modern computer were developed in the 1930s and 1940s. Computer were not
   commercially available until the 1950s.

5. There are several factory in my hometown. The glass factory employ many people.

6. Kangaroo are Australian animal. They are not on any of the other continent, except in zoo.

7. Mosquito are found everywhere in the world, including the Arctic.

8. At one time, many people believed that tomato were poisonous.

PRACTICE 5 ▸ Nouns as adjectives. (Chart 6-2)

Complete the sentences with the nouns in parentheses. Use the singular or plural form as appropriate.

1. (*project*) Julie manages _____projects_____ for her company. She's a _____project_____
   manager.

2. (*grocery*) They sell _____ at that store. It is a _____ store.

3. (*tomato*) I like _____ salads. I like salads that contain _____.

4. (*picture*) A friend gave us a wooden frame for _____. It's a very attractive wooden
   _____ frame.

5. (*flower*) I have a _____ garden. I grow several different kinds of
   _____.

6. (*drug*) Some people are addicted to _____. They are _____ addicts.

7. (*egg*) This carton holds one dozen _____. It's an _____ carton.

8. (*two + lane*) We drove down an old, narrow highway that had only _____. We drove down a _____ highway.

9. (*five + minute*) I gave a _____ speech in class. My speech lasted for _____.

10. (*sixty + year + old*) The Watkins family lives in a _____ house. Any house that is _____ usually needs a lot of repairs.

11. (*truck*) You need a special license to drive a _____. Ed has been a _____ driver for twenty-five years.

12. (*computer*) Susan programs _____. There are good jobs for _____ programmers everywhere.

13. (*peanut*) Emily has a _____ allergy. She is allergic to _____.

PRACTICE 6 ▶ Nouns as adjectives. (Chart 6-2)

Choose the correct completions.

1. A table in a kitchen is a _____.
   a. kitchen table   b. table kitchen   c. kitchen's table

2. The two tables in my bedroom are my _____.
   a. bedrooms tables   b. tables bedroom   c. bedroom tables

3. Scott has an office at his home. It's a _____.
   a. office home   b. home office   c. office of home

4. A lot of people have offices in their homes. They have _____.
   a. home offices   b. homes offices   c. homes office

5. I am out of food for my dog. I need a bag of _____.
   a. dogs food   b. dog food   c. food dog

6. There is a sink in the kitchen and one in each bathroom. We have two bathrooms. So we have one kitchen sink and two _____.
   a. bathrooms sinks   b. bathroom sink   c. bathroom sinks

7. In the back of our house, we grow vegetables in a garden. It's a _____.
   a. vegetable garden   b. vegetables garden   c. garden vegetables

8. We have two trees that grow cherries. They are _____.
   a. tree cherries   b. cherry trees   c. cherries trees

9. Joy and Don have a house by the beach. They have a _____.
   a. beach house   b. house beach   c. beaches house

10. That store sells chargers for phones. It sells _____.
    a. charger phone   b. phones charger   c. phone chargers

PRACTICE 7 ▶ Nouns as adjectives. (Chart 6-2)

Complete the sentences. Write the correct phrase using the two nouns in blue.

1. That handbook is for students. It is a _____*student handbook*_____.

2. There was a party to celebrate Lynn's birthday. There was a _____ for Lynn.

3. The retirees receive checks from the government every month. They receive a

   _____ every month.

4. The seats in the airplane are very small. The _____ are very small.

5. The pajamas are made of cotton. They are _____ .

6. There were no rooms in the local hotels that were available. There were no available

   _____ .

7. Their baby is ten months old. They have a _____ .

8. Our trip lasted for three days. We took a _____ .

9. Their apartment has three rooms. It is a _____ .

10. The professor asked us to write a paper of five pages. She asked us to write a

    _____ .

11. Luigi is a singer. He sings in operas. He's a famous _____ .

12. A convention for people who collect stamps is being held at City Center. My uncle is a collector.

    He has been a _____ since he was a boy.

PRACTICE 8 ▸ Possessive nouns. (Chart 6-3)
Answer the questions.

1. My parents' house is over 100 years old.

   a. What is the possessive noun? _____

   b. How many parents are there, one or more than one? _____

   c. What two nouns does the possessive (s') connect? _____ + _____

2. Safety is a parent's concern.

   a. What is the possessive noun? _____

   b. How many parents are there, one or more than one? _____

   c. What two nouns does the possessive ('s) connect? _____ + _____

3. Cats' eyes shine in the dark.

   a. What is the possessive noun? _____

   b. How many cats are there, one or more than one? _____

   c. What two nouns does the possessive (s') connect? _____ + _____

4. My cat's eyes are big and green.

   a. What is the possessive noun? _____

   b. How many cats are there, one or more than one? _____

   c. What two nouns does the possessive ('s) connect? _____ + _____

5. Do you know Mary's brother?

   a. What is the possessive noun? _____

   b. What belongs to Mary? _____

   c. What two nouns does the possessive ('s) connect? _____ + _____

6. Do you know Mary's brothers?

    a. What is the possessive noun? _____

    b. What belongs to Mary? _____

    c. What two nouns does the possessive ('s) connect? _____ + _____

7. My brothers' team won the game.

    a. What is the possessive noun? _____

    b. How many brothers do I have, one or more than one? _____

    c. What two nouns does the possessive (s') connect? _____ + _____

8. My brother's team won the game.

    a. What is the possessive noun? _____

    b. How many brothers do I have, one or more than one? _____

    c. What two nouns does the possessive ('s) connect? _____ + _____

PRACTICE 9 ▶ Possessive nouns. (Chart 6-3)

Check (✓) the correct number for the words in blue.

1. The teacher's office is down the hall.   ☐ one   ☐ more than one

2. The teachers' office is down the hall.   ☐ one   ☐ more than one

3. My sisters' clothes are all over my bed.   ☐ one   ☐ more than one

4. I visited the boy's house.   ☐ one   ☐ more than one

5. I agree with the judges' decision.   ☐ one   ☐ more than one

6. The customer service representative must listen to the customers' complaints.   ☐ one   ☐ more than one

7. The professor discussed the student's assignment.   ☐ one   ☐ more than one

8. The flight attendant put the passenger's bags in the overhead compartment.   ☐ one   ☐ more than one

PRACTICE 10 ▶ Possessive nouns. (Chart 6-3)

Make the *italicized* nouns possessive by adding apostrophes and final **-s** / **-es**. Delete and change a letter if necessary.

1. a. He put the mail in his *secretary* 's_____ mailbox.

    b. There are three secretaries in our office. The *secretary* ies'_____ mailboxes are in the hallway.

2. a. Tom has two cats. The *cat* _____ food and water dishes are on a shelf in the laundry room.

    b. I have one cat. My *cat* _____ feet are white, but the rest of her is black.

3. a. My *supervisor* _____ names are Ms. Anderson and Mr. Gomez.

    b. Your *supervisor* _____ name is Ms. Wright.

4. a. My twin *baby* _____ eyes are dark blue, just like their father's eyes.

    b. My *baby* _____ eyes are dark blue, just like her father's eyes.

5. a. Olga's *child* _____ name is Olaf.

   b. José and Alicia's *children* _____ names are Pablo and Gabriela.

6. a. All of the performers in the play did well. The audience applauded the *actor* _____ excellent performances.

   b. An *actor* _____ income is uncertain.

PRACTICE 11 ▸ Possessive nouns. (Chart 6-3)
Choose the correct completions.

1. My   mother's / mothers'   name is Maria.

2. Both my   grandmother's / grandmothers'   names were Maria too.

3. The   teacher's / teachers'   class is so big that the students in the back of the room can't hear her when she talks.

4. My   bosses' / boss'   name is Carl.

5. An   employee's / employees'   wallet was found under a table at the   employee's / employees'   cafeteria yesterday.

6. Here's the directory for the department store: the   mens' / men's   department is on the first floor; the   women's / womens'   department is on the second floor; the   children's / childrens'   department is on the third floor. On the third floor, the   girl's / girls'   clothes are on the right side, and the   boy's / boys'   clothes are on the left side.

PRACTICE 12 ▸ More about expressing possession. (Chart 6-4)
Choose the correct sentence.

1. a. I was 20 minutes late for yesterday's chemistry class.
   b. I was 20 minutes late for the chemistry class of yesterday.

2. a. I knew I had made a big mistake when I saw my professor's face.
   b. I knew I had made a big mistake when I saw the face of my professor.

3. a. I missed important information about next week's final exam.
   b. I missed important information about the final exam of next week.

4. a. I was late because I had run into an old teacher. She is now the history department's chair.
   b. I was late because I had run into an old teacher. She is now the chair of the history department.

5. a. She told me about a job opening for an office's assistant in the history department.
   b. She offered me a job opening for an office assistant in the history department.

6. a. I'm interested in the job. I will fill out the application's form later today.
   b. I'm interested in the job. I will fill out the application form later today.

7. a. I also need to copy my classmate's chemistry notes today.
   b. I also need to copy the chemistry notes of my classmate today.

PRACTICE 13 ▸ Count and noncount nouns. (Chart 6-5)
Look at the *italicized* nouns. Write "C" above the count nouns and "NC" above the noncount nouns.

1. We bought a lot of *food*. We bought some *eggs*, *bread*, *milk*, *coffee*, and *bananas*.
   (NC food; C eggs; NC bread; NC milk; NC coffee; C bananas)

2. I get a lot of *mail*. I get some *letters*, *magazines*, *catalogs*, and *bills* almost every day.

3. *Euros*, *pounds*, and *dollars* are different kinds of *money*.

4. Alma doesn't wear much *jewelry*. She wears a *ring* and sometimes *earrings*.

5. A *language* consists of *vocabulary* and *grammar*.

6. We need some *furniture* for the patio: a *table*, six *chairs*, and an *umbrella*.

PRACTICE 14 ▸ Count and noncount nouns. (Charts 6-5 → 6-7)
Choose the correct completions.

1. Every day I learn some more new   word / words   in English.

2. Olga knows   an / some   American slang.

3. There are a lot of   car / cars   on the highway at rush hour.

4. We got here so fast! There wasn't   much / many   traffic on the highway.

5. I ate a tuna   sandwich / sandwiches   for lunch.

6. We got only   some / one   good picture on our trip.

7. That website contains   an / some   excellent information.

8. That is   a very / very   good news!

PRACTICE 15 ▸ Count and noncount nouns. (Charts 6-5 → 6-7)
Add final *-s* / *-es* to the nouns in *italics* if necessary. Do not add, omit, or change any other words. Some sentences have no errors.

1. Jackie has brown *hair* and gray *eye*ˢ.

2. My parents gave me some good *advice*.

3. I always drink *water* when I'm hot and thirsty.

4. Do winning athletes need *luck*?

5. Our country has made a lot of *progress* in the last 25 years.

6. How many *class* are you taking this semester?

7. There are some *message* in my voicemail. I need to check them.

PRACTICE 16 ▸ Count and noncount nouns. (Charts 6-5 → 6-7)
Choose the correct completions.

1. It takes   courage / a courage   to be an astronaut.

2. We bought   some / a   new clothing.

3. The baby needs a new pair of   shoe / shoes.

4. The garbage truck comes on Monday, Wednesday, and Friday mornings to pick up the
   garbage / garbages.

5. I ordered twelve   glass / glasses   from a site on the Internet. When they arrived, one
   glass / glasses   was broken.

6. Many people need to wear   glass / glasses   to see better. The lenses should be made of
   glass / glasses   that doesn't break easily.

7. I filled out a report for   some / a   lost luggage at the airport, but I'm not optimistic. I wonder if
   they find   much / many   lost suitcases.

8. Would you like to go out tonight? I don't have   much / many   homework, and I'd like to go out
   and have   some / a   fun.

9. Ireland is famous for its beautiful green   hill / hills.   Ireland has   a lovely / lovely   scenery, but it often has   a damp / damp   weather.

10. The four-leaf clover is a symbol of   a good / good   luck in Ireland.

PRACTICE 17 ▶ Expressions of quantity with count and noncount nouns. (Chart 6-8)
Cross out the expressions that <u>cannot</u> be used to complete the sentences. Item 1 has been started for you.

1. Isabel did ＿＿＿ work last Saturday.

   a. ~~three~~
   b. ~~several~~
   c. some
   d. a lot of
   e. too much
   f. too many
   g. a few
   h. a little
   i. a number of
   j. a great deal of
   k. hardly any
   l. no

2. Zach is planning ＿＿＿ projects for next month.

   a. three
   b. several
   c. some
   d. a lot of
   e. too much
   f. too many
   g. a few
   h. a little
   i. a number of
   j. a great deal of
   k. hardly any
   l. no

PRACTICE 18 ▶ Expressions of quantity with count and noncount nouns. (Chart 6-8)
Complete the sentences with **much** or **many**. Also write the plural forms of the nouns as necessary. In some sentences, you will need to circle the correct verb in blue.

1. How ＿＿＿ *many* ＿＿＿ ~~computer~~ *computers* are there in the language lab?

2. How ＿＿＿ *much* ＿＿＿ equipment is there in the language lab?

3. How ＿＿＿ *many* ＿＿＿ ~~child~~ *children*   is / (are)   in Ms. Thompson's class?

4. How ＿＿＿＿＿＿ tooth do babies usually have when they're born?

5. Ellen and Rick have traveled widely. They've visited ＿＿＿＿＿＿ country.

6. I don't know ＿＿＿＿＿＿ American slang.

7. Enrique hasn't made ＿＿＿＿＿＿ progress in learning to play the piano. That's because he doesn't spend ＿＿＿＿＿＿ time practicing.

8. How ＿＿＿＿＿＿ apps do you usually download a month?

9. My hair is frizzy today. There   is / are   too ＿＿＿＿＿＿ humidity in the air.

10. I haven't done ＿＿＿＿＿＿ reading lately.

11. There   is / are   so ＿＿＿＿＿＿ smog in Los Angeles yesterday that you couldn't see any of the hills or mountains from the city.

12. I didn't know ＿＿＿＿＿＿ grammar before I took this course.

13. How ＿＿＿＿＿＿ active volcano   is / are   there in the world today?

14. Politicians give ＿＿＿＿＿＿ speech during their careers

PRACTICE 19 ▸ Expressions of quantity with count and noncount nouns. (Chart 6-8)
Choose all the correct completions for each sentence.

1. Pat bought a few _____ at the art show.
   a. pictures
   b. photographs
   c. art
   d. ceramic bowls

2. Mike bought some _____ at the supermarket.
   a. milk
   b. orange
   c. magazines
   d. flashlight battery

3. There were several _____ on the plane.
   a. child
   b. people
   c. babies
   d. passenger

4. There was a little _____ on the table.
   a. food
   b. cream
   c. coffee
   d. sandwiches

5. We have plenty of _____ for everyone.
   a. food
   b. pizza
   c. drinks
   d. hot dog

6. Can you bring a couple of _____ with you when you come to the party?
   a. ice
   b. hamburger
   c. bottles of soda
   d. water

7. I don't have many _____ about this.
   a. thoughts
   b. knowledge
   c. ideas
   d. information

8. Do Charlie and Kate have much _____?
   a. problems
   b. children
   c. fun
   d. work

9. I know a number of _____.
   a. people
   b. things
   c. professors
   d. news

10. They don't have a great deal of _____.
    a. intelligence
    b. information
    c. facts
    d. education

PRACTICE 20 ▸ Using *a few* and *few*; *a little* and *little*. (Chart 6-9)
In each pair of sentences, check (✓) the sentence that has the *bigger quantity* of something.

1. a. We have a little money. _✓_

   b. We have little money. _____

2. a. They know few people. _____

   b. They know a few people. _____

3. a. She has very little patience. _____

   b. She has a little patience. _____

4. a. I speak some Spanish. _____

   b. I speak little Spanish. _____

5. a. Marta asked few questions. _____

   b. Marta asked a few questions. _____

PRACTICE 21 ▸ Using *a few* and *few; a little* and *little*. (Chart 6-9)
Choose the correct completions.

1. Belinda learned to skate very quickly. At first, she fell down _____ times, but now she very rarely falls down.
   a. few   b. a few   c. a little

2. The police didn't have a good description of the bank robber. _____ witnesses actually saw his face.
   a. Few   b. A few   c. Little

3. Please pass the cream. I like _____ cream in my coffee. It tastes better.
   a. a few   b. a little   c. very few

4. You'd better know the answers when Professor Simpson calls on you in class tomorrow. He has _____ patience with students who are not prepared.
   a. very little   b. very few   c. a little

5. Before the hurricane, the stores were crowded with people buying supplies. By the time I got to a store, _____ flashlight batteries were left, and _____ bottled water was available.
   a. very little / very few   b. very little / very little   c. very few / very little

6. Come over to our house tonight. Peter is bringing his guitar. He'll play _____ folk music, and we'll sing _____ old songs.
   a. few / little   b. a few / a little   c. a little / a few

7. To make this sauce, first cook _____ onions in _____ oil.
   a. few / little   b. a few / a little   c. little / few

PRACTICE 22 ▸ Using *a few* and *few; a little* and *little*. (Chart 6-9)
Without changing the meaning of the sentences, replace the *italicized* words with **a few, few, a little,** or **little.**

1. If you put ~~some~~ *a little* sugar on those berries, they will taste sweeter.

2. Many people live to be more than 100 years old, but only ~~some~~ *a few* people live to be 110 years old.

3. Many cities in the world have a population of over a million, and *some* cities have a population of more than ten million.

4. You might reach your goal if you put forth *some* more effort.

5. The professor lectured very clearly. At the end of the class, *not many* students had questions.

6. I have to go to the post office because I have *some* letters to mail.

7. Every day Max goes to his mailbox, but it is usually empty. He gets *almost no* mail.

8. My friend arrived in the United States *some* months ago.

9. I think you could use *some* help. Let me give you *some* advice.

10. Margaret likes sweet tea. She usually adds *some* honey to her tea. Sometimes she adds *some* milk too.

PRACTICE 23 ▸ Singular expressions of quantity: *one, each, every.* (Chart 6-10)
Choose the correct word in the box. Write the correct singular or plural form. Some words may be used more than once.

child	goose	neighbor	✓ state
chimpanzee	man	puppy	woman

1. There is only one _____state_____ in the United States that is completely surrounded by water: Hawaii.

2. One of the _____states_____ in the United States that shares a border with Canada is Vermont.

3. Our dog had six puppies. I wanted to keep them all, but I couldn't. I kept one of the _____, but I gave away the other five.

4. There were six puppies. One _____ was black and white, and five were all black.

5. The children enjoyed the zoo. One of the _____ wandered away from the group, but she was quickly found at the snack bar.

6. The children particularly liked watching the chimpanzees. One _____, a boy named Kevin, seemed to be having a conversation with one of the _____.

7. One of our _____ gave a welcoming party for a new family who had just moved to our neighborhood from Ecuador.

8. There were several men riding on motorcycles together. One _____ seemed to be their leader. He was riding in front of the group.

9. The geese are flying in a V-formation. One _____ is at the point of the V, apparently leading the whole flock.

10. Our book club consists of 15 women. One of the _____ was just elected mayor of our town.

PRACTICE 24 ▸ Singular expressions of quantity: *one, each, every.* (Chart 6-10)
Correct the errors in the *italicized* words. Not every sentence has an error.

1. According to the Constitution of the United States, *every persons* has certain rights.

2. One of *rights* is the right to vote.

3. Each of *states* is represented by two senators in the U.S. Senate.

4. *Each of* senator is elected for a six-year term.

5. The number of representatives in the House of Representatives depends on the population of *each state*.

6. For example, Nevada, one of the very *small state*, has only three representatives, but New York, a populous state, has 29 representatives.

7. Every one of *citizen* is eligible to vote for president, but not every *citizen* exercises this right.

8. In some countries, voting is compulsory. Every *citizens* must vote.

PRACTICE 25 ▸ Using *of* in expressions of quantity. (Chart 6-11)
Complete the sentences with *of* or **Ø**.

1. Several _____ my colleagues are going to the lecture at the library tonight.

2. I have several _____ colleagues who have Ph.D's.

3. Many _____ the houses in New Orleans were lost to the floods that occurred after Hurricane Katrina.

4. These days, _____ new houses are being built with stronger materials to withstand hurricanes.

5. A few _____ children are born with exceptional musical talent.

6. Some _____ the children in Mr. McFarlane's music class are playing in a recital.

7. Most _____ people like to hear compliments.

8. My cousin won a million _____ dollars on a game show.

9. Many _____ places in the world use wind as a source of energy. Some _____ these places supply energy to thousands _____ homes and businesses.

10. There was hardly any _____ rain this spring. As a result, hardly any _____ my flowers bloomed.

11. To form the plural of most _____ the words in English, we add an *-s* or *-es* at the end. Not every word forms its plural in this way, however. Some _____ words have irregular endings.

PRACTICE 26 ▸ Chapter review.
There is one error in each sentence. Correct the error.

1. Last month, my brother and I cleaned out my grandparents attic.

2. We found a lot of old stuffs.

3. There was boxes and boxes of books.

4. We even found a 100-years-old copy of *The Adventures of Tom Sawyer*.

5. My brother was looking for old comic books, but he didn't find much comics.

6. He found a little of my uncle's old toys.

7. It was hard works, but we had a lot of fun.

8. My grandmother was happy to have a clean attic, and I was happy to have some of her old dishes and furnitures.

9. One persons' junk is another person's treasure.

PRACTICE 27 ▸ Chapter review.

Complete the crossword puzzle. Use the clues under the puzzle and the words in the box. All the words in the puzzle are from the charts in Chapter 6. All the sentences are well-known sayings in English.

all	every	many	mice	some
an	man	men	one	two

Across

3. _____ good things must come to an end.

4. You can't make an omelet without breaking _____ eggs.

6. A _____ is known by his friends.

8. _____ cloud has a silver lining.

Down

1. _____ heads are better than one.

2. _____ picture is worth a thousand words.

3. _____ apple a day keeps the doctor away.

5. When the cat's away, the _____ will play.

6. Too _____ cooks spoil the broth.

7. Dead _____ tell no tales.

CHAPTER 7
Articles

PRACTICE 1 ▸ Preview.
Read the passage. Underline the 22 articles (*a, an, the*).

Worry Dolls

Worry dolls are tiny colorful dolls. They usually come in a group of six to eight dolls in a small wooden box. These dolls are a folk tradition from Guatemala. The dolls are about one-half inch tall. Guatemalan artisans use a short piece of wire to make a frame with legs, arms, a torso, and a head. The artisans wrap yarn around the frame for the shape, and they use pieces of traditional fabric for the costumes. In the folk tradition, children tell a worry to each doll before they go to bed. Then they put the dolls back in the box and close the lid. When the children wake up in the morning, the worries are gone. The dolls have taken away all of the worries.

PRACTICE 2 ▸ Indefinite and definite nouns. (Chart 7-1)
Decide if the nouns in blue are definite or indefinite.

1. I have a friend from Guatemala.   definite   indefinite

2. She makes worry dolls.   definite   indefinite

3. Every year she sells the dolls at a fair.   definite   indefinite

4. The fair is in June.   definite   indefinite

5. Last year I bought some worry dolls.   definite   indefinite

6. The dolls help me sleep at night.   definite   indefinite

PRACTICE 3 ▸ Using *some*. (Chart 7-1)
Insert *some* where possible.

1. Hanna is going to the store. *no change*
2. She's buying ˄ ingredients for a cake. *(some)*
3. She's making a cake for her roommate's birthday.
4. She invited friends over for a party tonight.
5. They will eat cake and listen to music.
6. Hannah's friend Michael is a photographer. He'll take pictures.

PRACTICE 4 ▸ Articles: indefinite nouns. (Chart 7-1)

Complete the sentences with *a, an,* or *some*.

1. I asked _____*a*_____ question.
2. The students asked _____*some*_____ questions.
3. I got _____*an*_____ answer.
4. I received _____ information.
5. Chess is _____ game.
6. The children played _____ games at the party.
7. I heard _____ news about the hurricane.
8. I read _____ newspaper.
9. My professor wrote _____ letter to the newspaper.
10. I wrote _____ email to my professor.
11. I got _____ mail from the university.
12. Susan left _____ things in her car.
13. Matt bought _____ printer.
14. The printer needs _____ ink.

PRACTICE 5 ▸ Articles: indefinite and definite nouns. (Chart 7-1)

Complete the sentences with *a, an, the,* or *Ø*. Capitalize where necessary.

1. INDEFINITE: I'm shopping for _____*Ø*_____ clothes this weekend.

   DEFINITE: _____*The*_____ clothes in that store are very expensive.

2. INDEFINITE: I need _____ shirt.

   DEFINITE: I will try on _____ shirt before I buy it.

3. INDEFINITE: Does this store have _____ fitting room?

   DEFINITE: _____ fitting room is in the back of the store.

4. DEFINITE: _____ size is too large.

   INDEFINITE: I am looking for _____ different size.

5. DEFINITE: _____ salesclerk is helpful.

   INDEFINITE: Have you seen _____ salesclerk? I need help.

6. DEFINITE: Where is _____ price tag on these shoes?

   INDEFINITE: These shoes do not have _____ price tag.

7. INDEFINITE: I have _____ coupon.

   INDEFINITE: _____ coupon is for 20% off.

PRACTICE 6 ▸ Articles: generic nouns. (Chart 7-2)
Check (✓) if the noun in blue is singular or plural. Also check (✓) the nouns that have a generic meaning.

	Singular	Plural	Generic	Specific
1. a. Dogs need a lot of attention.		✓	✓	
b. I'm taking the dog for a walk.				
2. a. Hamsters are popular house pets.				
b. A hamster is a rodent.				
3. a. A cat can jump up to five times its own height.				
b. The cat jumped onto a table.				
4. a. Animal shelters take stray, lost, or abandoned animals.				
b. I adopted a dog from the animal shelter.				

PRACTICE 7 ▸ Articles: generic nouns. (Chart 7-2)
Choose the correct completions. All of the sentences have a generic meaning.

1. a. The baseball / Baseball   is a popular sport.

   b. Athletes wear   the uniforms / uniforms.

2. a. A data analyst / Data analyst   collects, organizes, and interprets statistical information.

   b. The data collection / Data collection   is important to many businesses.

3. a. The clarinet / Clarinet   is a musical instrument. It is a wind instrument.

   b. The violin / Violin   is a string instrument.

4. a. A pecan / pecan   is a nut.

   b. The pecans / Pecans   grow in Texas.

5. a. A blog / Blog   is a discussion or informational website.

   b. The bloggers / Bloggers   write content for blogs.

6. a. A meme / meme   is a humorous image or video that is copied and spread on the Internet.

   b. The memes / Memes   are popular on social media websites.

PRACTICE 8 ▸ Descriptive information with definite and indefinite nouns. (Chart 7-3)
Check (✓) if the noun in blue is about a definite or specific noun.

1. a. I ordered the book my teacher recommended. __✓__

   b. I like books about historical events. _____

2. a. Vanessa has a job interview at a world-famous hospital. _____

   b. She is nervous about the interview at that hospital. _____

3. a. I get lost easily. Please draw me a map to your house. _____

   b. I didn't get lost. The map to your house really helped. _____

4. a. Rhonda and Caroline met for lunch at a restaurant in Lexington. _____

   b. Do you know of a good restaurant in Lexington? I'm traveling there next week. _____

5. a. There is the store I told you about. _____

   b. There is a new store downtown. _____

6. a. Mariko needs a grammar book. _____

   b. Did Daniel do the homework in the grammar book? _____

PRACTICE 9 ▸ Using articles. (Charts 7-1 → 7-3)

Complete the sentences with *a, an,* or ***the***.

1. A: Let's take _____ break. Do you want to go to _____ movie?

   B: That's _____ good idea. Which movie do you want to see?

   A: _____ movie at the Rialto Theater is a comedy. Let's see that one.

2. A: Who knows _____ answer to this question?

   B: I do!

3. A: Professor Li, I have _____ question about the assignment.

   B: What's your question?

4. A: There's _____ spot on my shirt!

   B: Here. Take out _____ spot with this spot remover.

5. A: Listen! I hear _____ noise! Do you hear it?

   B: Yes, I hear something.

6. A: What was _____ noise that you heard?

   B: I think it was _____ mouse.

   A: But we don't have any mice in _____ house!

   B: Well, maybe it was just _____ wind.

PRACTICE 10 ▸ General article usage. (Chart 7-4)

Complete the sentences with *a/an, the,* or **Ø**. Capitalize as necessary.

1. ___Ø___ Ḷightning is ___a___ flash of light. It is usually followed by ___Ø___ thunder.

2. Last night we had ___a___ terrible storm. Our children were frightened by ___the___ thunder.

3. _____ circles are _____ round geometric figures.

4. _____ circle with _____ slash drawn through it is an international

   symbol meaning "Do not do this!" For example, _____ circle in

   _____ illustration means "No Smoking."

5. _____ inventor of _____ modern cell phone was Dr. Martin Cooper.

   He made the first call on the first portable handset in 1973 when he was

   _____ employee of the Motorola company.

6. Frank Lloyd Wright is _____ name of _____ famous architect. He is _____ architect who designed the Guggenheim Museum in New York. He also designed _____ hotel in Tokyo. _____ hotel was designed to withstand _____ earthquakes.

7. There was _____ small earthquake in California last year. _____ earthquake caused damage to several buildings, but fortunately, no one was killed.

PRACTICE 11 ▸ General article usage. (Chart 7-4)
Read each conversation. Choose the sentence that explains what the speakers are talking about.

1. A: Where's the teacher? I have a question.

   B: I'm not sure.
      a. Speaker A is asking about any teacher.
      b. Speaker A is asking about a teacher Speaker B is familiar with.

2. A: I put down the phone and now I can't find it.

   B: Oh, no!
      a. Speaker A is referring to a phone Speaker B is familiar with.
      b. Speaker A is referring to any phone.

3. A: Could you pick up some eggs and rice at the store? We'll have the rice for dinner.

   B: Sure.
      a. In the first sentence, *rice* is general. In the second sentence, *rice* is specific.
      b. In both sentences, *rice* is specific.

4. A: Bananas have a lot of potassium.

   B: They're very healthy.
      a. Speaker A is referring to a specific group of bananas.
      b. Speaker A is referring to bananas in general.

5. A: Does Saturn have a moon that orbits it?

   B: I don't know!
      a. Speaker A is talking about a specific moon.
      b. Speaker A is talking about any moon.

6. A: Have you seen the moon tonight?

   B: Yes! It's spectacular.
      a. The speakers are referring to the moon that goes around the Earth.
      b. The speakers are referring to any moon in the solar system.

PRACTICE 12 ▸ Using *the* or Ø with titles and geographic names. (Chart 7-5)
Complete the sentences with *the* or Ø.

1. _____ Doctor Kennedy moved from _____ United States to _____ Switzerland last year.

2. Some day I'll go to _____ Himalayas and climb _____ Mount Everest.

3. Pat and Laura went kayaking on _____ Colorado River.

4. _____ Canada borders three oceans. Canada's west coast is on _____ Pacific Ocean. To the north lies _____ Arctic Ocean. The east coast is on _____ Atlantic Ocean.

5. Jeff and Susanna traveled to _____ Europe for their honeymoon.

6. A: Have you ever been to _____ Caribbean Islands?

   B: Yes. I went scuba diving in _____ Jamaica a few years ago.

7. _____ Professor Bartels speaks Dutch. She is from _____ Netherlands.

8. _____ Austin is the capital city of _____ Texas.

PRACTICE 13 ▸ Chapter review.
Choose the correct completions.

Louis Braille was born in   the / Ø   France in 1809. He lost his eyesight due to   the / an   accident when he was   a / Ø   child. When he was 15 years old, he developed   a / Ø   writing system for   the / Ø   blind. The / A   writing system consists of   the / Ø   raised dots. The number and patterns of   the / some   dots form characters. The / A   system is called "Braille" after   the / an   inventor. Braille has spread from   the / Ø   France to many countries around   the / Ø   world.

PRACTICE 14 ▸ Chapter review.
Correct the errors.

1. It's beautiful today. Sun is shining and sky is clear.

2. I read good book about globalization.

3. The penguins live in Antarctica. The polar bears don't live in Antarctica.

4. Which is more important — the love or the money?

5. A: What does this word mean?

   B: Do you have dictionary? Look up word in dictionary.

6. A: Watch out! There's a bee buzzing around!

   B: Where? I don't see it. Ouch! It stung me! I didn't see bee, but I felt it!

7. Kevin is going to grocery store. He's getting some ingredients for a pasta dish.

8. Every summer Yoko's family goes camping in Canadian Rockies, but this summer they're going to beach instead.

PRACTICE 1 ▸ Preview.

Read the passage. In the parentheses after the pronoun, write the antecedent.

Selfie Sticks

A selfie stick holds a camera or smartphone on a pole. It enables

people to take a photograph of themselves (_____*people*_____)

1

from wide angles. Selfie sticks have become very popular.

They (_____*selfie sticks*_____) are taking the place of tripods. Many people

2

prefer selfie sticks over tripods because they (_____)

3

are easier to set up. They are also less expensive. The traditional way to take a "selfie," or a picture of

yourself, is to hold the camera yourself. Photography expert Amanda Campbell does not recommend

this method. She (_____) explains that your hands usually shake when you

4

are taking a selfie, so it (_____) will turn out blurry. People often drop and break their

5

(_____) cell phones when they are taking selfies. There are many good benefits to selfie

6

sticks. *Time* magazine called selfie sticks "the greatest invention of 2014."

    However, many opponents do not like selfie sticks. They (_____)

7

do not like to see people constantly posing in front of their own camera. Selfie sticks can also be

dangerous. One man caused an accident when he (_____) used his selfie stick on a

8

roller coaster. Because Disneyland is worried about accidents, it (_____) has banned

9

selfie sticks in its (_____) parks worldwide. Many museums have also banned them

10

(_____). They (_____) do not want visitors to bump into important

11   12

works of art as they (_____) try to take the perfect selfie. The *New York Times* called

13

selfie sticks "the most controversial gift of 2014."

PRACTICE 2 ▸ Personal pronouns. (Chart 8-1)

Draw a circle around each pronoun that has an antecedent. Draw an arrow from the pronoun to its antecedent.

1. Bob works for Trans-Ocean Airlines. (He) flies cargo across the Pacific Ocean.

2. Mr. and Mrs. Nobriega are moving. They have bought a house in the suburbs.

3. There goes my English teacher. Do you know her?

4. The baby just began to walk. She is eleven months old.

5. A new kind of car is being advertised. It runs on a battery.

6. There are two hawks up there on the telephone wire. Do you see them?

7. Sorry, Mr. Frank is not in the office now. Please call him at home.

8. We have a dog and a cat. They are part of our family.

PRACTICE 3 ▸ Personal pronouns. (Chart 8-1)
Choose the correct completions.

1. Sarah and   I / me   are taking a yoga class.

2. I'm going to tell you something, but don't tell anyone. It's just between you and   I / me.

3. Carlos and Julia were at the movies together. I saw   they / them.   They / Them   were holding hands.

4. Where are my papers? I left   it / them   right here on the table.

5. I have   my / mine   problems, and you have   your / yours.

6. Jim and Helena both work from home. He works at   he / his   computer all day, and she works
   at   her / hers.   At five o'clock sharp they both stop   they / their   work.

7. My aunt is only five years older than I am.   She and I / Her and me   are very close. We are like
   sisters.   Our / Ours   friends and relatives treat   our / us   like sisters.

8. I studied Latin when I was in high school. Of course, nobody speaks Latin today, but Latin was
   very useful to   me / I.   Because I understand   it / its   grammar, I can understand grammar in
   other languages. And my vocabulary is bigger because of   it / its   too.

9. When baby giraffes are born,   they / its   are six feet tall, taller than the average person.   They / It
   sometimes grow an inch a day, and they double   its / their   height in one year.

10. Did you know Mauna Kea in Hawaii is actually the tallest mountain in the world? If you measure it
    from   its / it's   base at the bottom of the Pacific Ocean to   its / it's   peak, it has a height of 33,476 feet
    10,203 meters.   Its / It's   taller than Mount Everest.

PRACTICE 4 ▸ Personal pronouns: agreement with generic nouns and indefinite pronouns. (Chart 8-2)
Choose the correct completions. In some sentences, both choices are correct.

1. All students must bring _____ books to class every day.
   a. his   b. their

2. Each girl in the class must bring _____ books to class every day.
   a. her   b. his or her

3. Everyone on the tennis team must leave _____ cell phone number with the coach.
   a. his or her   b. their

4. Everybody on the men's bowling team brings _____ own bowling ball to the bowling alley.
   a. his   b. his or her

5. Everyone should know how to do _____ job.
   a. his or her   b. their

6. Girls, whose keys are these? Somebody left _____ keys on the table.
   a. their   b. her

7. Nobody in the Boy Scout troop failed _____ tests. Everybody passed.
   a. his   b. their

PRACTICE 5 ▸ Personal pronouns: agreement with collective nouns. (Charts 8-2 and 8-3)
Complete the sentences with a word or phrase in the box. You may use an item more than once.

her	his or her	its	them
his	it	their	they

1. Tonight's audience is special. Everyone in _____ is a member of the fire department or the police department. The show is being performed especially for _____ .

2. When the play was over, the audience arose from _____ seats and applauded wildly.

3. The actors bowed to the audience's applause. The leading man took _____ bow first, and then the leading lady took _____ bow.

4. The faculty of the philosophy department is very small. In fact, _____ has only two professors. _____ share an office.

5. Well, Mia, I'm sorry you're having problems. Everyone has _____ problems, goodness knows!

6. A notice sent home with each girl on the girls' volleyball team said: "The girls' volleyball team is playing at Cliffside on Friday of this week. This will be _____ final game of the season. Each girl must have a signed consent form for a field trip from _____ mother or father."

7. Instructions on an application for admission to a university said: "Each student must submit _____ application by December 1st. The admissions committee will render _____ final decision before April 1st."

PRACTICE 6 ▸ Reflexive pronouns. (Chart 8-4)
Complete the sentences with the appropriate reflexive pronouns.

1. In our creative writing class, we all had to write short biographies of ___*ourselves*___ .

2. Anna wrote a biography of _____ .

3. Tom wrote a biography of _____ .

4. Larry and Harry, who are twins, wrote biographies of _____ , but surprisingly, they were not similar.

5. I wrote a biography of _____ .

6. After our teacher had read them all, he asked us, "Did all of you enjoy writing about _____ ?"

7. One student replied. He said, "Well, yes, I think we did. But now we would like to know something about you. Will you tell us about _____ ?"

PRACTICE 7 ▸ Reflexive pronouns. (Chart 8-4)

Complete the sentences with one of the words or phrases in the box, and add a reflexive pronoun.

feeling sorry for	help	✓ is angry at	pat
fix	introduce	laugh at	talks to

1. John overslept and missed his plane to San Francisco. Now he
   _____ *is angry at himself* _____ for not checking his alarm clock before going to bed.

2. I didn't know anyone at the party. I stood alone for a while; then I decided to walk over to an
   interesting-looking person and _____ to him.

3. Sue, please _____ to some more cake. And would you like
   some more coffee?

4. You did a great job, team. You should all _____ on the back for
   playing the game so well.

5. Sabrina is a lonely little girl. She doesn't have any brothers or sisters, or live near any friends.
   Sometimes she _____ or to an imaginary friend.

6. The sink is not going to _____. We have to call a plumber to do it.

7. Come on, Kim. Don't be so hard on yourself. Everyone makes mistakes. We have to
   _____ sometimes and keep a sense of humor!

8. I told Tommy he couldn't buy a new toy today. He's mad at me. He's in his bedroom
   _____.

PRACTICE 8 ▸ Using *you*, *one*, and *they* as impersonal pronouns. (Chart 8-5)

Choose the correct completions.

1. People make New Year's resolutions at the beginning of a new year. They promise _____ that they
   will do something to improve their well-being, or to benefit their community or the world.
   a. them   b. oneself   c. themselves

2. One should be honest with _____.
   a. one   b. oneself   c. yourself

3. Parents tell their children, "You should be polite to _____ elders."
   a. your   b. one's   c. their

4. How do _____ start this car?
   a. you   b. one   c. he

5. How does _____ make a complaint in this store? Is there a customer-service department?
   a. you   b. they   c. one

6. If you are a student, _____ can get a discount at shops in the mall.
   a. they   b. you   c. one

7. Students can get discounts at the mall. _____ just have to show their student ID.
   a. They   b. Themselves   c. One

PRACTICE 9 ▸ Forms of *other*. (Chart 8-6)

Choose the correct completions.

1. One of the biggest problems in the world is global warming. _____ problem is AIDS.
   a. Another   b. The another   c. Other

2. Some cities have strict anti-pollution laws, but _____ cities do not.
   a. other   b. others   c. the others

3. New York is a multilingual city. In addition to English, many people speak Spanish. _____ speak French, Chinese, Portuguese, or Russian.
   a. Others   b. Other   c. Another

4. In addition to these languages, there are 40 _____ languages spoken in New York City, according to the U.S. Census Bureau.
   a. other   b. others   c. another

5. Istanbul lies on both sides of the Straits of Bosporus. One side is in Europe, and _____ side is in Asia.
   a. another   b. the other   c. other

6. There are 47 countries in Africa. Of these, 35 countries have coastlines. _____ do not have coastlines; they are landlocked.
   a. Others   b. The other   c. The others

7. There are several countries that have a king or a queen. One is Thailand. _____ is England.
   a. Another   b. The other   c. The another

8. There are a few _____ countries that have a king or a queen, but I can't remember which ones.
   a. others   b. other   c. another

9. Scandinavia consists of four countries. One is Denmark. _____ are Finland, Norway, and Sweden.
   a. The other   b. The others   c. Others

10. Canada has ten provinces. French is the official language of Quebec province. English is the language of _____ provinces.
    a. others   b. another   c. the other

11. Washington is one of the five states of the United States with borders on the Pacific Ocean. What are _____ states?*
    a. other   b. the other   c. the others

PRACTICE 10 ▶ Forms of *other*. (Chart 8-6)
Choose the correct completions.

1. A: How much longer until we get home?

   B: We're almost there. We have   other / another   20 minutes.

2. A: This road is expensive! I see we have to pay more money at the next toll booth.

   B: Right. I think we have to pay   another / others   three dollars.

3. A: So you didn't buy that house way out in the country?

   B: No, it's too far from work. I have to drive ten miles to work now. I don't want to add   another / the another   ten miles to the trip.

4. A: I heard you moved out of your apartment.

   B: That's right. They raised the rent by 100 euros. I didn't want to pay   other / another   100 euros.

5. A: How was the test?

   B: I am sure that I failed. I didn't finish. I needed   other / another   ten or fifteen minutes to finish.

6. A: Who won the game?

   B: The other team. In the last minute of the game, our team scored six points, not enough to win; we needed   another / other   eight points.

PRACTICE 11 ▸ Common expressions with *other*. (Chart 8-7)

Complete the sentences in Column A with a phrase from Column B.

Column A

1. John loves Mary and Mary loves John. They love ____.

2. Nobody in my class understands this poem ____ Ron, who seems to understand everything.

3. The discussion group doesn't meet every week; it meets ____ week, that is, twice a month.

4. A tiger is a feline; ____, it's a cat, a big cat.

5. The children jumped into the water one by one, in a line, ____.

6. What? The letter carrier quit his job? I saw him just ____. He seemed happy.

Column B

a. every other

b. one after another

c. the other day

d. each other

e. in other words

f. other than

PRACTICE 12 ▸ Review. (Chapters 6–8)

Read the passage and correct the errors.

Cyber Security

Who are hackers?

Hackers look for weaknesses in a computer system. They use the weaknesses to break into computer systems or computer networks. Some hackers break into computer systems because he enjoys the challenge. The others work for large companies. These companies hire hackers to find weaknesses and point it out. Afterwards, the companies fix the weaknesses. Another hackers have criminal motivations. These hacker create viruses and worms. They steal important informations, such as the passwords and bank account numbers.

What are viruses and worms?

A computer virus is piece of code. Viruses attach themself to files and programs. They copy themself and spread to each computers they come in contact with. They often spread through email messages or Internet downloads. Some viruses slow down computers. Anothers completely disable computers.

Worms are similar to viruses, but they do not need to attach to a files or programs. Worms use networks to send copies of its code to others computers.

How can you protect your devices?

There are much ways to protect your devices. To start with, keep your firewall on. A firewall is software program or piece of hardware. It protects your device from hackers. Second, install anti-virus software. This software finds and removes viruses and worms. Next, keep your operating system up to date. Newer operating systems have fixed a lot of the security problem from the old versions. Finally, don't open an attachments or download anything from a unfamiliar person.

PRACTICE 1 ▸ Preview.
Read the passage. <u>Underline</u> the 10 modal verbs.

Applying to a University

Thank you for your interest in State University. You must meet certain
entrance requirements before you can apply for admission. Each
academic department has different requirements. You should read
the specific requirements for your major. All applicants must submit
a completed application form, entrance exam results, high school or
college transcripts, and an application fee.

You must submit your application electronically. All students must take at least one entrance exam.
Some majors may require more than one exam. The testing agency will send all entrance exam
results directly to the university. Your high school or college may send your transcripts electronically
or by mail in a sealed envelope. You may pay the application fee online with a credit card payment or
mail a check or money order to the Office of Admissions.

PRACTICE 2 ▸ Expressing necessity: *must, have to, have got to* (Chart 9-2)
Choose the correct completions. More than one answer may be possible.

1. The application deadline is next week. I _____ to submit my application as soon as possible.
   a. must   b. have got   c. has

2. Sarah and I are taking our entrance exam tomorrow. We _____ arrive at the testing center by 9:00 A.M.
   a. must   b. have got   c. have to

3. We _____ to bring identification, such as a driver's license, to the testing center.
   a. must   b. have got   c. have

4. Sarah doesn't have a driver's license. She _____ bring her passport instead.
   a. must   b. has to   c. have to

5. Have you taken the entrance exam yet, or do you still _____ take it?
   a. must   b. has to   c. have to

PRACTICE 3 ▸ Expressing lack of necessity and prohibition. (Chart 9-3)
Complete the sentences with ***must not*** or ***don't have to***.

1. a. We _____ do tonight's homework. It is extra credit work.

   b. We _____ turn in our homework late. The professor does not accept late work.

2. a. You _____ park in a fire lane. It is prohibited.

   b. You _____ park this far away. There are plenty of open spaces near the building.

3. a. The university does not allow smoking in the campus buildings. You _____ smoke within 25 feet of any campus building.

b. I can read the "No smoking" signs. You _____ tell me.

4. a. We _____ stay in the library past 10:00. It closes at that time.

b. The library is open tomorrow, but it is a school holiday. We _____ be on campus.

PRACTICE 4 ▸ Expressing necessity, lack of necessity, and prohibition. (Charts 9-2 and 9-3)
Read the statements. Then check (✓) the box that describes each item.

	Necessity	Lack of Necessity	Prohibition
1. Taxpayers must pay their taxes by April 15th.	✓		
2. You must not touch electrical wires.			
3. Students don't have to register on campus. They can register by computer.			
4. We've got to hurry! We don't want to miss our flight!			
5. You don't have to pay for the car all at once. You can pay month by month.			
6. Passengers must show their boarding passes and their IDs when they go through security.			
7. A person has to be 17 years old to obtain a driver's license in many states.			
8. Doctors have to graduate from medical school and pass special exams before they can practice medicine.			
9. Soldiers must not disobey a superior officer.			
10. Nobody has to come to work tomorrow! The company has given everybody a day off.			

PRACTICE 5 ▸ Expressing necessity, lack of necessity, and prohibition. (Charts 9-2 and 9-3)
Choose the correct completions.

1. Plants _____ have water or they will die.
   a. must   b. don't have to   c. must not

2. A lot of people _____ leave their homes to go to work. They can work from their home offices.
   a. must   b. don't have to   c. must not

3. To stay alive, people _____ breathe oxygen.
   a. must   b. don't have to   c. must not

4. People who have diabetes will have serious health problems if they eat foods with a lot of sugar.

   They _____ eat foods with a lot of sugar.
   a. must   b. don't have to   c. must not

5. A salesperson _____ motivate people to buy his or her product.
   a. has to   b. doesn't have to   c. must not

6. You _____ finish your work on this project before you go on vacation. Your job is in danger.
   a. must   b. must not   c. don't have to

7. My room is a mess, but I _____ clean it before I go out tonight. I can do it in the morning.
   a. have got to   b. must not   c. don't have to

8. I _____ get some help with my statistics course. If I don't, I won't pass it.
   a. have got to   b. must not   c. don't have to

9. Yoko _____ study for her English tests. She understands everything without studying.
   a. has to   b. must not   c. doesn't have to

10. Everywhere in the world, stealing is against the law. People _____ steal.
    a. must   b. must not   c. don't have to

PRACTICE 6 ▸ Advisability: *should, ought to, had better.* (Chart 9-4)
Choose the sentence with the stronger meaning.

1. a. I should study.
   b. I'd better study.

2. a. You must turn right here.
   b. You should turn right here.

3. a. He's got to get a warmer jacket.
   b. He ought to get a warmer jacket.

4. a. You should get new tires for your car.
   b. You'd better get new tires for your car.

5. a. They shouldn't say those words.
   b. They must not say those words.

6. a. Jane had better not tell anyone about this.
   b. Jane shouldn't tell anyone about this.

7. a. You must not drink the water here.
   b. You shouldn't drink the water here.

8. a. We don't have to vote for John Turner.
   b. We shouldn't vote for John Turner.

PRACTICE 7 ▸ Advisability: should, ought to, had better. (Chart 9-4)
Cross out the ideas that are not good advice for each situation, or are not relevant to the situation.
More than one answer may be possible.

1. José wants to lose weight.
    a. He should exercise regularly.
    b. ~~He should eat a lot of sweets.~~
    c. He should go on a diet.

2. Ludmila wants to go to medical school in a few years.
    a. She should study poetry now.
    b. She should take science and math courses now.
    c. She should start saving money for tuition.

3. Ikira is a concert pianist.
    a. He should take good care of his hands.
    b. He should go bowling often.
    c. He should visit his grandmother often.

4. Mia is failing her math class.
    a. She should drink a lot of black coffee.
    b. She should get a tutor to help her.
    c. She should study more.

5. Beth wants her flowers to grow.
    a. She should water them.
    b. She should take a math class.
    c. She should give the flowers plant food as directed.

6. Ira sprained his ankle.
    a. He should practice standing on it.
    b. He should rest his ankle.
    c. He should put ice on it.

PRACTICE 8 ▸ Advisability: should, ought to, had better. (Chart 9-4)
Give advice to the people in the following situations. Write the letter of the piece of advice that fits each situation.

   a. call home and talk to his family quite often
   b. change his clothes before he goes
   c. clean it up right away
   d. get his roommate a set of earphones
   e. join some clubs to meet people with similar interests
   f. make her own decisions about her career
   g. stop for gas as soon as we see a station
   h. take it back now so you won't have to pay any more money

1. Ann would like to make some new friends. She should _____.

2. We're running out of gas! We had better _____.

3. Sam and Tim, both teenagers, have messed up the house, and their parents are coming home soon.
    They had better _____.

4. You are going to have to pay a fine because your library book is overdue. You ought to _____.

5. Ron is wearing jeans. He has to go to a wedding this evening. He had better _____.

6. Mary's parents expect her to work in the family business, a shoe store, but she is an adult and wants
    to be an architect. She should _____.

7. Richard's roommate, Charlie, stays up very late studying. While Charlie is studying, he listens to loud music, and Richard can't get to sleep. Richard ought to _____.

8. Pierre is feeling really homesick these days. He should _____.

PRACTICE 9 ▸ Expectation: *be supposed to*. (Chart 9-5)
Rewrite the sentences with a form of **be supposed to** + *verb*.

1. Allen is expected to arrive at seven o'clock.

   Allen _____ at seven o'clock.

2. I'm expected to go hiking with Beth on Saturday, but I'd really rather sleep late.

   I _____ hiking with Beth on Saturday, but I'd really rather sleep late.

3. The weather is expected to be nice over the weekend.

   It _____ nice over the weekend.

4. The plane was expected to arrive at 6:35, but it didn't.

   The plane _____ at 6:35, but it didn't.

5. I was expecting my friends to come over tonight, but they didn't.

   They _____ tonight, but they didn't.

6. Our dog is very independent. We expect him to run to us when we call his name, but he completely ignores us.

   Our dog _____ to us when we call his name, but he completely ignores us.

PRACTICE 10 ▸ Expectation: *should*. (Chart 9-5)
Rewrite the sentences in blue with **should**.

1. The movie has excellent reviews. **I expect it to be a good movie.**

   _____

2. The movie came out a year ago. **I expect it is available online now.**

   _____

3. It is a comedy. **I expect it to be funny.**

   _____

4. The lead actor appears in a new movie every year. **I expect he will appear in a new movie soon.**

   _____

PRACTICE 11 ▸ Ability: *can, know how to*, and *be able to*. (Chart 9-6)
Part I. Rewrite the sentences using **be able to**.

1. Kevin can speak four languages.

   _____

2. Please speak more loudly. I can't hear you.

   _____

3. Can you arrive early tomorrow?

   _____

4. I can understand your point of view.

   _____

Part II. Rewrite the sentences using *know how to*.

1. Ikuko can create a PowerPoint presentation.

   _____

2. Lucy failed her driving test. She can't parallel park.

   _____

3. Mazzen can code in JavaScript.

   _____

4. Can you fix my computer?

   _____

PRACTICE 12 ▸ Possibility: *can, may, might.* (Chart 9-7)
Complete the sentences with *can*, *may*, or *might* to express possibility.

1. I have a meeting tonight. I _____ be home late.

2. Joe _____ rent an apartment in the suburbs.

3. Apartments in the city limits _____ be very expensive.

4. Bring an umbrella. It _____ rain this afternoon.

5. I usually dress in layers in the spring. The weather _____ be cool.

PRACTICE 13 ▸ Polite requests with *I* as the subject; polite requests with *you* as the subject. (Chart 9-8)
Complete the sentences with a phrase in the box.

Can I help you	Could you please repeat
Can you hurry	May I borrow
could you help me	Would you please give me

1. A: Oh, no! I've lost my passport. Rick, _____ find it?

   B: OK. I'll be right there.

2. A: Oh, no! I've lost my passport.

   B: _____, Jenny? Maybe I can find it for you.

3. A: I'm sorry. Mr. Robbins isn't in today. Do you want to leave a message on his voicemail?

   B: Well, it's very important. _____ his cell phone number?

4. A: _____ your dictionary, please?

   B: Sure.

5. A: OK, sir. I'll be there sometime today to fix your refrigerator.

   B: _____, please? The frozen food is melting fast!

6. A: Students, do you understand the assignment?

   B: Not really, Dr. Johnson. _____ what you said?

PRACTICE 14 ▶ Polite requests with *Would you mind*. (Chart 9-9)
Complete the sentences with *if I* + the present tense or the *-ing* form of the verb.

1. a. I want you to cook dinner.   Would you mind _____*cooking*_____ dinner?

   b. I want to cook dinner.   Would you mind _____*if I cooked*_____ dinner?

2. a. We want you to take us to the airport. Would you mind _____ us to the airport?

   b. We want to take you to the airport.   Would you mind _____ you to the airport?

3. a. I want to open the windows.   Would you mind _____ the windows?

   b. I want you to open the windows.   Would you mind _____ the windows?

4. a. We want you to join us for lunch.   Would you mind _____ us for lunch?

   b. We want to join you for lunch.   Would you mind _____ you for lunch?

5. a. I want you to write a letter to the boss. Would you mind _____ a letter to the boss?

   b. I want to write a letter to the boss.   Would you mind _____ a letter to the boss?

PRACTICE 15 ▶ Polite requests with *Would you mind*. (Chart 9-9)
Complete the sentences with the verbs in parentheses. Write *if I* + the past tense or the *-ing* form of the verb. In some sentences, either response is possible, but the meaning is different.

1. A: It's cold in here. Would you mind (*close*) _____*closing*_____ the window?

   B: Not at all. I'd be glad to.

2. A: It's cold in here. Would you mind (*close*) _____*if I closed*_____ the window?

   B: Not at all. Go right ahead. I think it's cold in here too.

3. A: You're going to the library? Would you mind (*take*) _____ this book back to the library for me?

   B: Not at all.

4. A: I'm not feeling well at all. Would you mind (*go*) _____ home now?

   B: Oh, I'm sorry. I hope you can come back when you feel better.

5. A: I'm not feeling well at all. Would you mind (*leave*) _____ now before the visiting hours are over?

   B: Oh, of course not. We shouldn't stay more than a short time for a hospital visit anyway.

6. A: I'll be working late tonight, honey. Would you mind (*cook*) _____ dinner tonight? I'll clean up after dinner.

   B: I'd be happy to. About what time do you think you'll be home?

7. A: We have a lot of chicken left over from dinner last night. Would you mind (*make*) _____ a chicken salad from the leftovers for dinner tonight?

   B: No, that'll be good. You make a great chicken salad.

8. A: I'm exhausted. Chopping wood in the hot sun is hard on me. Would you mind

(*finish*) _____ the work yourself?

B: No problem, Grandpa. Why don't you go in and rest? I'll finish up.

9. A: Would you mind (*use*) _____ your name as a reference on this job application?

B: Not at all. In fact, ask them to call me.

10. A: I'd like to apply for the job as department manager. Would you mind

(*recommend*) _____ me to the boss?

B: No. As a matter of fact, I was thinking of recommending you myself.

PRACTICE 16 ▸ Making suggestions: *let's, why don't, shall I / we.* (Chart 9-10)
Choose the correct completions. More than one answer may be possible.

1. _____ we go out for dinner tonight?
   a. Shall   b. Why do   c. Let's   d. Why don't

2. _____ home and watch a movie.
   a. Why not staying   b. Let's stay   c. Why not we stay   d. Shall stay

3. Why _____ the teacher for help?
   a. you not ask   b. don't you ask   c. you ask   d. don't you to ask

4. It's cold in this room. _____ the window?
   a. Why don't I close   b. Shall I close   c. Let's closing   d. I shall

5. Why don't we _____ for lunch tomorrow?
   a. meeting   b. meets   c. meet   d. met

6. _____ go out tonight. I have a test in the morning.
   a. Let's don't   b. Let's not   c. Let's no   d. Don't lets

PRACTICE 17 ▸ Chapter review.
Correct the modal verb errors.

1. Our teacher can to speak five languages.

2. Oh, this table is heavy! Jim, may you help me move it?

3. We come to class on weekdays. We are not have to come to class on weekends.

4. Park here. It's free. You must not pay anything.

5. When you speak in front of the judge, you must to tell the truth. You must not tell lies.

6. Pat looks tired. She should gets some rest.

7. I not able to go to the party this weekend.

8. The children are suppose to be in bed by nine o'clock.

9. The Garcias supposed to be here at 7:00, but I think they will be late, as usual.

10. We're going to make chicken for dinner. Why you don't join us?

11. Here's my advice about your diet, Mr. Jackson. You could not eat a lot of sugar and salt.

12. A: This is wonderful music. Will we dance?

B: No, let's don't dance. Let's just sit here and talk.

PRACTICE 1 ▶ Preview.

Read the passage. <u>Underline</u> the four modals.

A Surprise Victory

Last Friday's soccer match should have been an easy game for the Wildcats. Their team had an undefeated record this season. However, fans couldn't believe it when the Falcons defeated the Wildcats 5-2. It was the first win of the season for the Falcons. The Falcons must have practiced very hard to achieve their surprise victory. The next Falcons game is this Friday at 6:00 P.M. on their home field. It should be an exciting game!

PRACTICE 2 ▶ Repeated action in the past. (Chart 10-1)

Complete the sentences with **would** or **used to** and a verb in the box. Use **would** when possible. Use any words in parentheses.

bring	fall	listen	say	stay	throw
come	have	live	sleep	tell	wipe

1. I'll always remember Miss Emerson, my fifth-grade teacher. Sometimes a student

   _____ asleep in her class. Whenever that happened, Miss Emerson

   _____ a piece of chalk at the student!

2. My father never liked to talk on the phone. Whenever it rang, he

   (*always*) _____, "I'm not here!" Usually, he was only joking and

   _____ to the phone when it was for him.

3. I have fond childhood memories of my Aunt Betsy. Whenever she came to visit, she

   (*always*) _____ me a little present.

4. My uncle Oscar _____ with us when I was a child. He had some strange habits.

   For example, he (*always*) _____ his plate with his napkin whenever

   he sat down to a meal.

5. When I was in college, I _____ some bad habits. I didn't study until the night

   before a test, and then I _____ up all night studying. Then the next day after

   the test, I _____ all afternoon.

6. I'll never forget the wonderful evenings I spent with my grandparents when I was a child. My

   grandmother _____ stories of her childhood seventy years ago, and we

   _____ intently and ask a lot of questions.

PRACTICE 3 ▸ Past tense of *must* and *have to*. (Chart 10-2)
Rewrite the sentences using the past tense.

1. You must use blue ink on the form.

   _____

2. The students have to memorize 100 new words a week.

   _____

3. Sylvia has to cancel her summer vacation plans.

   _____

4. Who do you have to call?

   _____

5. The children must get vaccinations.

   _____

6. The passengers have to fasten their seat belts because of the turbulent weather.

   _____

PRACTICE 4 ▸ The past form of *should*. (Chart 10-2)
Give advice about the situation using the past form of ***should***. Complete each sentence with a verb in the box. Use any words in parentheses.

buy	come	order	take	visit
change	keep	stay	turn	watch

1. A: We're having hamburgers? I thought you were cooking a turkey for the holiday.

   B: I did, but I cooked it for too long. It burned up in the oven! I _____
   it out after three hours, but I forgot.

2. A: Where are we? Are we lost?

   B: I think we are. We _____ left instead of right at the last intersection.

3. A: I'm tired this morning! What time did we finally go to bed last night?

   B: Around 2:00 A.M. We (*not*) _____ that late movie.

4. A: Is Lionel angry at you?

   B: He is. I _____ his mother when she was so sick, but I didn't.

5. A: Beautiful shoes! Where did you buy them?

   B: I bought them at Norwalk's, but I _____ them online. They were
   a lot cheaper there.

6. A: How was dinner at Henri's?

   B: Not so good. I had the fish, but it didn't taste fresh. I _____
   something else.

7. A: Why are you upset with Frank?

   B: He came to work today with a terrible cold, coughing and sneezing all over us! He

   (*not*) _____ to work today.

   He _____ home.

8. A: Are you glad you took the new job?

   B: No, actually, I'm not. I (*not*) _____ jobs.

   I _____ my old job.

PRACTICE 5 ▸ Present and past forms of *should*. (Chart 10-2)

Give advice in each situation. Complete each sentence with the present or past form of **should** and the verb in parentheses.

1. Travel teaches us about the world. Everyone (*travel*) _____.

2. We did not travel to Africa when we had the opportunity last year.

   We (*go*) _____ at that time.

3. Our house will look much better with a fresh coat of paint. It will look good in a yellow

   color. I think we (*paint*) _____ our house, and the color

   (*be*) _____ yellow.

4. We painted our house. Now it's white and has beige shutters. It doesn't look good. We

   (*not, paint*) _____ our house in such dull colors.

5. Ernie is allergic to shellfish. Last night he ate shellfish, and he broke out with terrible hives. Ernie

   (*not, eat*) _____ that shellfish.

6. Some people are sensitive to caffeine. They cannot fall asleep at night if they drink coffee in the

   afternoon. These people (*not, drink*) _____ coffee after 12:00 P.M. They

   (*drink*) _____ decaffeinated coffee or tea instead.

7. Years ago, people did not realize that some species were dying off because of human activity. For

   example, many buffalo in North America were killed because of human thoughtlessness. As a result,

   there are few buffalo left in North America. People (*not, kill*) _____

   those buffalo.

8. Today, people are making efforts to save the environment and to save endangered species. We

   (*make*) _____ strong efforts to recycle, conserve our resources, and

   nourish endangered species.

PRACTICE 6 ▸ Past forms of *be supposed to*. (Chart 10-2)

Rewrite the sentences. Use a form of **be supposed to** + *verb*.

1. The plane was expected to arrive at 6:35, but it didn't.

   The plane _____ at 6:35, but it didn't.

2. I was expecting my friends to come over tonight, but they didn't.

   They _____ tonight, but they didn't.

3. I was expecting to give a presentation in class today, but we ran out of time.

   I _____ a presentation in class today, but we ran out of time.

4. Weather forecasters expected it to snow today, but it didn't.

It _____ today, but it didn't.

5. Did your teacher expect you to turn in your essay today?

_____ your essay today?

PRACTICE 7 ▶ Ability: *can* and *could*. (Chart 10-3)
Complete the sentences with *can, can't, could,* or *couldn't.*

1. Fish _____ talk.

2. My uncle was a wonderful craftsman. He made beautiful things out of wood. But he

_____ read or write because he never went to school.

3. A bilingual person _____ speak two languages.

4. I _____ get to sleep last night because it was too hot in my room.

5. Why _____ all the nations of the world just get along in peace? Why are there always

wars somewhere on earth?

6. When I was younger, I _____ stay up past midnight and get up at dawn feeling ready

to go. I _____ do that any longer now that I'm middle-aged.

7. I was sitting in the back of the classroom today. I _____ hear the professor.

_____ I borrow your notes?

PRACTICE 8 ▶ Degrees of certainty: present time. (Chart 10-4)
How certain is the speaker when making each of the following remarks? Check (✓) the appropriate box.

	100%	About 95%	About 50% or less
1. Charlotte might be home by now.			✓
2. Phil must be home now.			
3. Mr. Brown's at home now.			
4. Lilly must know the answer to this question.			
5. Fred might have the answer.			
6. Shelley knows the answer.			
7. Those people must have a lot of money.			
8. You may remember me from high school.			
9. We could be related!			
10. Traffic might be heavy on the interstate.			

PRACTICE 9 ▸ Degrees of certainty: present time. (Chart 10-4)
Choose the correct completions. In some sentences, both answers are correct.

1. A: Drive slowly! This is a school zone. Children are crossing the street here.

   B: It _____ be three o'clock. That's the time that school is out.
   a. must   b. might

2. A: Professor McKeon says that we're going to have a very high inflation rate next year.

   B: He _____ be right. He knows more about economics than anyone I know.
   a. must   b. could

3. A: Have you heard anything from Ed? Is he still on safari in Africa?

   B: He _____ be, or he _____ already be on his way home. I'm just not sure.
   a. must ... must   b. may ... may

4. A: Is that a famous celebrity over there in the middle of that crowd?

   B: It _____ be. She's signing autographs.
   a. must   b. might

5. A: Isn't Peter Reeves a banker?

   B: Yes. Why don't you talk to him? He _____ be able to help you with your loan.
   a. must   b. may

6. A: Is Margaret's daughter 16 yet?

   B: She _____ be. I saw her driving a car, and you have to be at least 16 to get a driver's license.
   a. must   b. might

7. A: Overall, don't you think the possibility of world peace is greater now than ever before?

   B: It _____ be. I don't know. Political relationships can be fragile.
   a. must   b. may

8. A: What's the matter with my son, doctor? Why does he cough and sneeze every day?

   B: He's allergic to something. It _____ dust in the house, or certain foods, or pollen in the air, or something else. It's hard to know, so we'll do some tests to find out.
   a. must be   b. may be

9. A: The speedometer on my car is broken. Do you think I'm driving over the speed limit?

   B: I can't tell. It doesn't seem like it, but you _____.
   a. must be   b. could be

10. A: You've been on the go all day. Aren't you exhausted?

    B: Yes, I _____. I can't remember when I've ever been this worn out.
    a. am   b. must be

11. A: I thought this movie was a comedy!

    B: Me too, but it _____ sad. Look at the people leaving the theater. A lot of them are crying.
    a. might be   b. must be

12. A: How old do you think Roger is?

    B: I just saw his driver's license. He _____ 33.
    a. could be   b. is

PRACTICE 10 ▸ Degrees of certainty: present time negative. (Chart 10-5)
Complete the sentences with the correct phrase in the box.

a. can't be him	d. may not speak
b. can't be true	e. must not get
c. may not be	f. must not like

1. A: I can't hear the singers! That man sitting behind us is snoring in his sleep!

   B: I hear him! He _____ opera.

2. A: Look! Isn't that our history professor over there? In the yellow sweater!

   B: No, that _____. He's in Tokyo this week, giving a presentation.

3. A: This coffee doesn't taste very good. It's supposed to be 100% Arabica.

   B: It _____ 100% Arabica. Maybe they mixed it with something else. Maybe it's a blend.

4. A: Who is that woman standing alone over there? She isn't talking to anyone.

   B: Well, she _____ any English. Or maybe she's very shy. Anyway, let's go over and try to talk to her.

5. A: Jane has been accepted at Harvard, I heard.

   B: No way! That _____. She isn't even a good student.

6. A: Did you see the new pickup truck that Mario's driving?

   B: I sure did. It's very big. It _____ good gas mileage.

PRACTICE 11 ▸ Degrees of certainty: past time. (Chart 10-6)
Choose the sentence that describes the given sentences.

1. The little boy is crying. His knees are scraped and bleeding.
   a. He may have fallen down.
   b. He must have fallen down.

2. Someone called, but I don't know who it was. Maybe it was Alice, but I'm not sure.
   a. It may have been Alice.
   b. It must have been Alice.

3. Nobody's answering the phone at Juan's apartment. I guess he has already left for the airport.
   He always likes to get to the airport early, you know.
   a. He might have already left for the airport.
   b. He must have already left for the airport.

4. I've lost track of my old friend Lola from high school. Maybe she moved away. Maybe she got
   married and has a different last name.
   a. She could have moved away.
   b. She must have moved away.

5. Irv looks unhappy today. Maybe his boss criticized him. Maybe he had an argument with his
   girlfriend. Maybe he lost a lot of money in the stock market.
   a. Irv might have had an argument with his girlfriend.
   b. Irv must have had an argument with his girlfriend.

6. I told Charles — only Charles — about my secret engagement, but now everyone is congratulating
   me! It's clear that Charles can't keep a secret.
   a. Charles may have told everyone.
   b. Charles must have told everyone.

PRACTICE 12 ▶ Degrees of certainty: past time negative. (Chart 10-6)
Write the past negative of an appropriate modal and the verb in parentheses.

1. ANN: I've called Howard ten times, I'm sure. He doesn't answer his cell phone.

    SAM: He (*remember*) _____ you were going to call him.
    He's a little forgetful, you know. I'll bet he forgot to turn his phone on.

2. LAWYER: Mr. Jones, where were you on the night of June 24th?

    MR. JONES: I was at home. I was at home all night.

    LAWYER: You (*be*) _____ at home on that night, Mr. Jones.
    Four witnesses saw you at the victim's apartment.

3. JIM: Look! There are lights on in the Thompsons' house. Didn't they go away on vacation?

    ANN: They (*leave*) _____ yet. Or maybe they left the automatic
    timer on to deter burglars.

4. BOB: Hey, you guys! You are not supposed to ride your bikes on the sidewalk! You could crash
    into someone!

    SUE: They (*hear*) _____ you, Bob. Look! They just kept going.

5. Scientists are not sure why the Mayan civilization collapsed. The Mayans
    (*have*) _____ enough to eat, or perhaps their enemies became
    too strong for them.

6. After his voyage on the *Kon Tiki*, Thor Heyerdahl set forth the theory that modern Polynesians
    descended from ancient South Americans. However, later scientists believe this
    (*happen*) _____. They believe it was impossible because of
    recent DNA evidence to the contrary.

PRACTICE 13 ▶ Degrees of certainty: present and past time. (Charts 10-4 → 10-6)
Complete the conversations with **must** and the verb in parentheses. Use the correct present or past
form. Use **not** if necessary.

1. A: You got here in 20 minutes! You (*drive*) _____ really fast. Normally
    it's a 40-minute drive.

    B: No faster than usual.

2. A: Sally gave a speech at her graduation. I think I saw tears in her parents' eyes.

   B: Oh, that is touching. They (be) _____ very proud of her.

3. A: That's strange. Oscar didn't come to the meeting. He never misses a meeting.

   B: He (know) _____ about it. He was out of town all last week, and

   probably no one told him.

4. A: How old do you think our teacher is?

   B: Well, she was a couple of years ahead of my father in college, so she

   (be) _____ around 55 now.

5. A: Uh-oh! I can't find my credit card.

   B: You (leave) _____ it at the cash register at the grocery store.

6. A: Have you seen Clark? I can't find him anywhere.

   B: He was feeling terrible. He (go) _____ home a while ago.

7. A: Look! Do you see that big bird on top of the tree?

   B: What big bird?

   A: You can't see that? You (need) _____ stronger glasses.

8. A: What happened to your knee?

   B: I twisted it very badly in the tennis match.

   A: Oh! That (hurt) _____ a lot!

PRACTICE 14 ▸ *Must have* vs. *had to*. (Charts 9-2 and 10-6)
Choose the correct response.

1. ANN: Why didn't you come to the party?
   BOB: a. I had to study.   b. I must have studied.

2. SAM: Where's Sally? She's still not here?
   DAN: a. She must have overslept.   b. She had to oversleep.

3. IRA: Thomas missed an important meeting this morning.
   JAN: I just spoke with him and he's very sick. He told me he . . .
       a. had to go to the doctor's.   b. must have gone to the doctor's.

4. BOB: We're out of coffee again.
   TOM: a. Jane must have forgotten to get some.   b. Jane had to forget to get some.

5. PAT: How were you able to stay awake during that long, boring lecture?
   ONA: It was difficult!
       a. I must have drunk a lot of coffee! b. I had to drink a lot of coffee!

6. LIL: I can't sleep again!
   MAX: a. You must have drunk too   b. You had to drink too
       much coffee today.   much coffee today.

PRACTICE 15 ▸ Degrees of certainty: future time. (Chart 10-7)
Complete the sentences in Column A with a phrase from Column B.

Column A

1. Keiko has always loved animals. She's in veterinary school now. She should _____.

2. Most apple trees bear fruit about five years after planting. Our apple tree is four years old. It should _____ next year.

3. Aunt Ella's plane arrived an hour ago. She's taking a taxi, so she should _____.

4. We could invest this money in a conservative stock fund. If we do that, we should _____ at the end of a year.

5. Ali should _____. He's been studying hard for it all semester.

6. The little horse is growing very fast. He should _____ in a year.

7. Bake the fish in the oven at 350 degrees. It should _____ in about ten minutes.

8. Take this medicine every morning. You should _____ in about two weeks.

9. Luis is taking a heavy course load. He wants to finish school quickly. He should _____.

10. The mechanic is fixing the car now. It should _____.

Column B

a. be here just in time for dinner

b. do very well on the final exam

c. feel better

d. double his weight

e. make a great veterinarian

f. have about 5% more

g. be fixed before five o'clock

h. graduate next June

i. be moist and tender

j. give us some apples

PRACTICE 16 ▸ Degrees of certainty: future time. (Chart 10-7)
Choose the correct completions.

1. Today is Monday. Tomorrow should / will be Tuesday.

2. Hello, Jack. This is Arturo in the tech department. I'm working on your computer now. Good news — I can fix it pretty easily and it should / must be ready by 5:00 P.M. today.

3. My son's birthday is next month. He should / will be two years old.

4. It's ten minutes to four. The next bus must / should arrive at four o'clock. The buses usually stop here every hour on the hour.

5. A: Don't be late! They won't let you into the theater after the play begins.
   B: OK. I will / should be at the theater at 7:15. I promise.

6. Your husband is resting comfortably, Ms. Robbins. I'm giving him some antibiotics, so the infection must / should clear up quickly.

7. A: Look up there. Is that Mars?
   B: I don't think so. Mars isn't visible right now. It should / must be Venus. Venus is visible now.

8. A: Who's going to win the tennis tournament?
   B: Well, the Australian is highly rated, and she must / should win, but the Serbian is good too. Maybe she'll surprise us and win.

PRACTICE 17 ▸ Progressive forms of modals. (Chart 10-8)

Complete the sentences. Use the appropriate progressive forms of *must, should,* or *may / might / could* and a verb in the box. You may use a verb more than once.

date	fly	hike	kid	sleep	work

1. A: Call Phil. He's at his office now.

   B: Let's email him instead. He _____ on something important at the moment. Or maybe he's with a client.

2. A: When will Betty be back from Italy?

   B: Tonight. She _____ over the Atlantic at this very moment.

3. A: Helga must know the answer to this problem. Shall we call her?

   B: Not now. It's 11:00 P.M. She _____.

4. A: Listen, I just heard this. Mr. Milner isn't going to be our teacher anymore. He has joined the army.

   B: You _____! That can't be true. Who told you that?

5. A: Sara told me that she had won the lottery, and so she invited us all to dinner at Henri's French restaurant.

   B: Oh, she _____ when she said that. She never plays the lottery!

6. A: What do you think Ann's doing now on her vacation?

   B: Oh, she _____ in the mountains. Or maybe she's relaxing at the pool.

7. A: I was hoping to go out with John, but I heard he's dating Julia.

   B: Well, he (*not*) _____ Julia anymore. I think that they may have broken up.

PRACTICE 18 ▸ Combining modals with phrasal modals. (Chart 10-9)

Complete each sentence with the given words. Write the words in their correct order in the sentences.

1. to \ get \ have

   You _____ *have to get* _____ a passport if you are going to travel in other countries.

2. be \ should \ to \ able \ complete

   Everyone _____ this form easily.

3. have \ to \ won't \ stand

   People _____ in the line for a long time. The line is moving quickly.

4. you \ be \ able \ leave \ to \ will

   When _____ here?

5. not \ able \ to \ graduate \ to \ going \ am \ be

   I _____ with my class. I lost a complete semester when I was sick.

6. been \ must \ to \ get \ have \ not \ able

   Mike and Helen haven't arrived yet. They were going to try to get on an earlier flight. They _____ on the earlier flight.

PRACTICE 19 ▸ Expressing preference: *would rather.* (Chart 10-10)

Complete the sentences with a form of **would rather** and a verb in the box. Use any words in parentheses.

eat	go	have	sail	say	study

1. I know you want to know, but I (*not*) _____ anything more about this topic. I told Marge that I'd keep it a secret.

2. Last night, I _____ home right after dinner at the restaurant, but my friends insisted on going back to John's apartment to listen to some music and talk.

3. I _____ history and literature in college than study business as I did. I majored in business, and now that's all I know. I might never again have the opportunity to learn about history and literature.

4. If you insist, we'll go to the pizza place after the movie, but I

   (*not*) _____ pizza again. I'm tired of it.

5. Do you think that young people _____ a choice about whom to marry, or do you think that they prefer their parents to choose a partner for them?

6. I like my work a lot, but my favorite thing is sailing. I love sailing. At this moment, even though I have just been promoted to vice-president of my company, I _____ right now instead of sitting here in my office.

PRACTICE 20 ▸ Chapter review.

Choose the correct completions.

1. A: Where's Angie? Didn't she come back after lunch?

   B: I'm not sure where she is. But she _____ the presentation that Human Resources is giving right now.
      a. is attending   b. could attend   c. could be attending

2. A: You're taking Spanish at 8:00 A.M. every day? Why did you choose such an early class?

   B: Because Ms. Cardenas is the teacher. She _____ excellent. I've been in the class for a month now, and I don't mind the early hour.
      a. should be   b. must be   c. is

3. A: The meteorologists predicted five major hurricanes for this hurricane season.

   B: They _____ wrong, you know. Sometimes they make mistakes.
      a. must be   b. might be   c. are

4. A: Is this chicken in the refrigerator still good?

   B: I don't think so. It's been in there for over a month! It _____ spoiled by now.
      a. may be   b. must be   c. could be

5. A: Can you tell me if Flight 86 is on time?

   B: It is on time, sir. It _____ at Gate B21 in about five minutes.
      a. might arrive   b. might be arriving   c. should be arriving

6. A: Did you know that Mike got a scholarship to State School of Engineering?

   B: Yes, I know that! I was the first one he told about it. He _____ very happy.
      a. might be   b. must be   c. is

7. A: Did you know that Li received a scholarship to the City School of Music?

   B: No, I didn't. That's great news! He _____ very happy.
      a. might be   b. must be   c. is

8. A: Who's going to win the election?

   B: It's a close call. The senator _____ with all his experience, but the opposition candidate is stronger than anyone expected.
      a. must win   b. must be winning   c. should win

9. A: Where's Harold? He's supposed to be at this meeting. Didn't Jim tell him about it?

   B: Jim _____ to tell him.
      a. must forget   b. must have forgotten   c. should have forgotten

10. A: This soup has an interesting flavor, but there's too much salt in it.

    B: Yes, it is too salty. I _____ so much salt in it.
       a. must not have put   b. shouldn't have put   c. may not have put

PRACTICE 21 ▶ Chapter review.
Write modal sentences for the situations.

1. The plane is late, and we didn't call the airport.

   a. I expect it will arrive soon. _____*It should arrive soon.*_____

   b. Maybe it took off late. _____*It may / might / could have taken off late.*_____

   c. It was a good idea to call the airport, but we didn't. _____*We should have called the airport.*_____

2. There's a package in the mail. _____

   a. Maybe it's for me. _____

   b. I'm sure it's for me. _____

   c. It's impossible that it's for me. _____

3. Tom didn't respond to my email.

   a. I expected him to respond. _____

   b. Maybe he didn't get it. _____

   c. I'm pretty sure he didn't get it. _____

   d. His email isn't working. It was impossible for him to get it. _____

4. There's water all over the kitchen floor.

   a. Perhaps the dishwasher is leaking. _____

   b. The dishwasher is new. It's impossible that it's the dishwasher. _____

   c. I'm pretty sure a pipe is broken. _____

   d. It's a good idea for you to call a plumber. _____

   e. It isn't necessary for us to call a plumber. _____

Read the following passage. Choose all of the possible completions in parentheses.

Distracted Drivers

Distracted drivers often cause major traffic accidents. In the past, before the widespread use of smartphones, drivers   would / could / should   be distracted by eating, reading maps, or grooming. These activities   can / could / might   still cause problems, but one of the biggest issues today is cell phone use. People   can / might / must   use their phones to talk, text, engage in social media, play games, use navigation systems, check their bank accounts, write shopping lists, listen to music, or look up information on the Internet.

Joy has become a leading advocate against distracted driving since she had an accident last year. She hit another car and blacked out. She   can't / couldn't / shouldn't   remember anything about the accident. According to her phone records, she   must have been / must be / must have   talking on the phone when the accident occurred. Luckily, no one was injured. It   could have been / must have been / can have been   much worse. She still feels terrible about the accident. She   shouldn't have been using / shouldn't have used / shouldn't used   her phone while she was driving.

Advocates like Joy are calling for stricter distracted-driving laws. Several places have already adopted laws against texting or using a cell phone at all while driving. With more distracted-driving laws, the roads   should / can / may   become much safer.

CHAPTER 11

The Passive

PRACTICE 1 ▶ Preview.
Read the passage. <u>Underline</u> the seven passive voice verbs.

School Closing

The National Weather Service has issued a winter storm warning. Heavy snowfall is expected early this evening. More than a foot of snow is anticipated by tomorrow morning. Because student safety is our top priority, classes have been canceled for the remainder of the day. The university's business offices are also closed. Residence and dining halls will remain open. Tonight's basketball game has been postponed to next Tuesday. Classes will be canceled all day tomorrow. The university is monitoring the weather closely and will notify the campus community with any additional updates. More details can be found on our school website.

PRACTICE 2 ▶ Forming the passive. (Charts 11-1 and 11-2)
Change the active to the passive by writing the correct form of *be*. Use the same tense for *be* in the passive sentence that is used in the active sentence.

Mrs. Bell answered my question. My question _____*was*_____ **answered** by Mrs. Bell.

1. *simple present:*

    Authors write books. .... Books _____ **written** by authors.

2. *present progressive:*

    Mr. Brown is writing that book. .... That book _____ **written** by Mr. Brown.

3. *present perfect:*

    Ms. Lee has written the report. .... The report _____ **written** by Ms. Lee.

4. *simple past:*

    Bob wrote that letter. .... That letter _____ **written** by Bob.

5. *past progressive:*

    A student was writing the report. .... The report _____ **written** by a student.

6. *past perfect:*

    Lucy had written a memo. .... A memo _____ **written** by Lucy.

7. *simple future:*

    Your teacher will write a report. .... A report _____ **written** by your teacher.

8. *be going to:*

   Tom is going to write a letter. .... The letter _____ **written** by Tom.

9. *future perfect:*

   Alice will have written the report. .... The report _____ **written** by Alice.

10. The judges have made a decision. .... A decision _____ **made** by the judges.

11. Several people saw the accident. .... The accident _____ **seen** by several people.

12. Ann is sending the letters. .... The letters _____ **sent** by Ann.

13. Fred will plan the party. .... The party _____ **planned** by Fred.

14. The medicine had cured my illness. .... My illness _____ **cured** by the medicine.

15. The cat will have caught the mouse. .... The mouse _____ **caught** by the cat.

16. Engineers design bridges. .... Bridges _____ **designed** by engineers.

17. The city is going to build a bridge. .... A bridge _____ **built** by the city.

18. A guard was protecting the jewels. .... The jewels _____ **protected** by a guard.

PRACTICE 3 ▶ Active vs. passive. (Charts 11-1 and 11-2)

<u>Underline</u> the subject of each sentence. Circle the complete verb. Then identify the sentences as active
(A) or passive (P).

1. a. __A__ <u>Henry</u> (visited) a national park.

   b. __P__ <u>The park</u> (was visited) by over 10,000 people last month.

2. a. _____ Olga was reading the comics.

   b. _____ Philippe has read all of Tolstoy's novels.

   c. _____ *Bambi* has been read by children all over the world.

3. a. _____ Whales swim in the ocean.

   b. _____ Whales were hunted by fishermen until recently.

4. a. _____ The answer won't be known for several months.

   b. _____ I know the answer.

5. a. _____ Two new houses were built on our street.

   b. _____ A famous architect designed the new bank on First Street.

6. a. _____ The Internet was invented before I was born.

   b. _____ The Internet has expanded the knowledge of people everywhere.

7. a. _____ The World Cup is seen on TV all over the world.

   b. _____ Soccer fans all over the world watch the World Cup on TV.

PRACTICE 4 ▸ Forming the passive. (Chart 11-2)

Complete the sentences. Change the verbs in blue from active to passive.

1. Alex writes the book.   →   The book _____*is written*_____ by Alex.
2. Alex is writing the book.   →   The book _____ by Alex.
3. Alex has written the book.   →   The book _____ by Alex.
4. Alex wrote the book.   →   The book _____ by Alex.
5. Alex was writing the book.   →   The book _____ by Alex.
6. Alex had written the book.   →   The book _____ by Alex.
7. Alex will write the book.   →   The book _____ by Alex.
8. Alex is going to write the book. → The book _____ by Alex.
9. Alex will have written the book. → The book _____ by Alex.
10. Did Alex write the book?   →   _____ the book _____ by Alex?
11. Will Alex write the book?   →   _____ the book _____ by Alex?
12. Has Alex written the book?   →   _____ the book _____ by Alex?

PRACTICE 5 ▸ Forming the passive. (Chart 11-2)

Part I. Complete the sentences. Change the verbs from active to passive.

1. Picasso painted that picture.

    That picture was _____*was painted by Picasso*_____.

2. Experienced pilots fly these planes.

    These planes _____.

3. A famous singer is going to sing the national anthem.

    The national anthem _____.

4. Yale University has accepted my cousin.

    My cousin _____.

5. The doctor will examine the patient.

    The patient _____.

6. The defense attorney is questioning a witness.

    A witness _____.

7. A dog bit our mail carrier.

    Our mail carrier _____.

8. The mother bird was feeding the baby bird.

    The baby bird _____.

9. His words won't persuade me.

    I _____.

10. I didn't paint this picture. Did Laura paint it?

    The picture _____.

    Was it _____?

11. Does Mrs. Crane own this restaurant? I know that her father doesn't own it anymore.

Is this restaurant _____?

I know that it _____.

12. I didn't sign these papers. Someone else signed my name.

These papers _____.

My name _____.

Part II. Change each sentence to the active voice. The subject of the new sentence is given. Keep the same tense of the verb.

1. My teeth are going to be cleaned by the dental assistant.

The dental assistant _____.

2. Was that email sent by Mr. Tyrol?

_____ Mr. Tyrol _____?

3. The Fourth of July isn't celebrated by the British.

The British _____.

4. Has your house been sold by the realtor yet?

_____ the realtor _____?

5. The thief hasn't been caught by the police.

The police _____.

6. The carpets are being cleaned by the carpet cleaners.

The carpet cleaners _____.

PRACTICE 6 ▸ Active vs. passive. (Charts 11-1 and 11-2)
Check (✓) the incorrect sentences.

_____ 1. I wasn't surprised by his message.

_✓_ 2. Accidents are happened every day.

_____ 3. The plane was arrived at nine.

_____ 4. Towels are supplied by the hotel.

_____ 5. Jill's essay was published in a magazine.

_____ 6. Are ghosts existed?

_____ 7. Mr. Lee was died last year.

_____ 8. It hasn't been rained lately.

_____ 9. The speech was delivered by a young politician.

_____ 10. The actress has been appeared in three films this year.

_____ 11. The error was noticed by everyone.

_____ 12. The meeting has been postponed until next week.

PRACTICE 7 ▶ Active vs. passive. (Charts 11-1 and 11-2)

Choose the correct completions.

1. We'll let you know about the job. You _____ by my secretary next week.
   a. will notify   b. will be notified   c. will have notified

2. Last night I _____ to lock my front door.
   a. wasn't remembered   b. didn't remember   c. hadn't been remembered

3. This old wooden desk _____ by my grandfather over 40 years ago.
   a. built   b. had built   c. was built

4. Disneyland is a world-famous amusement park in Southern California. It _____ by millions of people every year.
   a. is visited   b. visited   c. has visited

5. I _____ with people who say space exploration is a waste of money. What do you think?
   a. not agree   b. don't agree   c. am not agree

6. Do you really think that we _____ by creatures from outer space in the near future?
   a. will invade   b. be invaded   c. will be invaded

7. Had you already _____ by this university when you heard about the scholarship offer from the other school?
   a. were accepted   b. accepted   c. been accepted

8. When Jason was only ten, his father _____.
   a. was died   b. died   c. dead

9. Elephants _____ a long time, sometimes for 70 years.
   a. live   b. were lived   c. have been lived

10. The impact of the earthquake yesterday _____ by people who lived hundreds of kilometers from the epicenter.
    a. felt   b. has felt   c. was felt

11. At one time, the entire world _____ by dinosaurs.
    a. ruled   b. was ruled   c. been ruled

12. Some dinosaurs _____ on their hind legs and were as tall as palm trees.
    a. walked   b. were walked   c. have stood

PRACTICE 8 ▶ Using the passive. (Chart 11-3)

Choose the sentence that has the same meaning as the given sentence.

1. In my dream, the monster is being chased.
   a. The monster is chasing someone in my dream.
   b. Someone is chasing the monster in my dream.

2. An airplane was delivered to a cargo facility last week.
   a. The airplane delivered some cargo.
   b. Someone delivered the airplane.

3. Witnesses are going to be asked for information.
   a. Someone will request information from witnesses.
   b. Witnesses will request information from someone.

4. Internet access will be provided free of charge.
   a. The Internet will provide access.
   b. Someone will provide Internet access.

5. All of the participants have been counted.
   a. Someone has finished counting the participants.
   b. The participants have finished counting.

PRACTICE 9 ▸ Using the passive. (Chart 11-3)

Complete each passage with the given verbs. Write the correct form of the verb, active or passive.

1. invent / tell

   The sandwich _____ by John Montagu, an Englishman with the title of

   the Earl of Sandwich. Around 1762, he was too busy to sit down at a regular meal, so he

   _____ his cook to pack his meat inside some bread in order to save him time.

2. attend / establish / give

   Al-Azhar University in Cairo, Egypt, is one of the oldest universities in the world. It

   _____ around the same time as the city of Cairo, in 969 A.D. The first

   lecture _____ in 975 A.D. Students (*still*) _____ the university today.

3. become / kill / know / live / relate / save

   One animal that is famous in the history of the American West is actually a bison, but it

   _____ by the name of *buffalo*. The American buffalo _____

   to a similar animal in Asia, the water buffalo. Buffaloes _____ in parks and

   flat grasslands. At the end of the nineteenth century, they almost _____

   extinct because thousands of them _____ by hunters. Fortunately, they

   _____ by the efforts of naturalists and the government.

4. believe / give / like / originate / treat / use / value

   Garlic _____ in Asia over 6,000 years ago, and it spread throughout Europe

   and Africa. Today, people _____ to use garlic not only for its strong flavor, but

   because it _____ them physical strength and good health. In ancient times,

   garlic _____ so highly that it _____ as money. Injuries

   and illnesses _____ with garlic by the ancient Greeks. Even today, garlic

   _____ to be effective by some people in lowering cholesterol and in treating

   other digestive disorders.

PRACTICE 10 ▸ Active vs. passive. (Charts 11-1 → 11-3)

Write complete sentences with the given words. Use the simple past.

1. the chefs \ prepare \ the food ___*The chefs prepared the food*_____.

2. the food \ prepare \ yesterday ___*The food was prepared yesterday*_____.

3. the rain \ stop _____.

4. a rainbow \ appear \ in the sky _____.

5. the documents \ send \ to you \ yesterday _____.

6. my lawyer \ send \ the documents to me _____.

7. the winner of the election \ announce \ on TV _____.

8. I \ not agree \ with you about this _____.

9. what \ happen \ yesterday _____?

10. something wonderful \ happen \ to me _____.

11. the trees \ die \ of a disease _____.

12. the trees \ kill \ by a disease _____.

13. a disease \ kill \ the trees _____.

14. I \ accept \ at the University of Chicago _____.

15. I \ recommend \ for a scholarship _____.

PRACTICE 11 ▸ The passive form of modals and phrasal modals. (Chart 11-4)
Choose the correct completions.

1. A language   can't be / couldn't have been   learned only by reading about it. You have to practice speaking it.

2. These jeans   should be washed / should have been washed   before you wear them. The material will be softer and more comfortable.

3. This shirt was washed in hot water, and it shrank. It   should have washed / should have been washed   in cold water.

4. The road is still being fixed. It is supposed   to be finished / to finish   by next month, but I'm not so sure it will be.

5. There's an old house for sale on Route 411. They say that George Washington visited it, so it   must be built / must have been built   in the 1700s.

6. Taxes   have to pay / have to be paid   on or before April 15th. Payments   must be sent / must have been sent   to the government on or before April 15th.

7. The senator has made a good point, but I disagree. May I   permit / be permitted   to speak now?

8. Our kitchen is old and dark. We're going to renovate it. It   ought to be painted / ought to paint   a light shade of green or white to make it look brighter.

PRACTICE 12 ▸ The passive form of modals and phrasal modals. (Chart 11-4)
Complete the sentences with the words in parentheses. Write the appropriate form, active or passive.

1. a. The decision (should + make) _____ as soon as possible.

   b. We (should + make) _____ our decision right now, without further discussion.

2. a. A decision (should + make) _____ before now.

   b. We (should + make) _____ our decision weeks ago.

3. a. I agree with you completely. Truer words (couldn't + speak) _____.

   b. They say that Einstein (couldn't + speak) _____ until he was four years old.

4. a. All vehicles (must + register) _____ with the Department of Motor Vehicles of this state.

   b. You (must + register) _____ your car with the Department of Motor Vehicles.

5. a. This bill (have to + pay) _____ by tomorrow.

   b. I (have to + pay) _____ this bill online. I can't mail a check, or it won't get there in time.

6. a. Someone called, but they hung up. It (*must + be*) _____ a wrong number.

   b. There (*may + be*) _____ life on Mars long ago.

PRACTICE 13 ▸ Stative (non-progressive) passive. (Chart 11-5)
Complete the sentences in Column A with a verb from Column B.

Column A	Column B
1. Uh-oh. I forgot my key, and the door is _____.	a. finished
2. The museum isn't open today. It's _____.	b. lost
3. Finally! The report I've been writing for a week is _____.	c. crowded
4. The TV doesn't work. It's _____.	d. turned on
5. Do you know where we are? I think we're _____.	e. closed
6. Let's go to another restaurant. This one is too _____.	f. gone
7. What happened to the cookies? They're all _____.	g. locked
8. It's freezing in this room! I guess the heat isn't _____.	h. broken

PRACTICE 14 ▸ Stative (non-progressive passive). (Charts 11-5 and 11-6)
Complete the sentences with the verbs in the box. Use the present tense, active or passive. Add a preposition if necessary.

bore	depend	interest	make	prepare
compose	equip	locate	marry	scare

1. Ismael _____ the history of languages. He is studying linguistics.

2. We may have a picnic on Saturday. It _____ the weather.

3. Sam _____ Salma. They have been married for 24 years.

4. Our son _____ the dark, so we keep a night light on in his room.

5. Golf _____ me. There isn't any action, and it is too slow.

6. These jeans _____ cotton. They're 100% organic cotton.

7. Our class is diverse. It _____ people from nine countries.

8. The Hague _____ the Netherlands.

9. The lab _____ the latest technology.

10. I've been studying all weekend. I _____ my exam.

PRACTICE 15 ▸ Common non-progressive (stative) passive verbs + prepositions.
(Chart 11-6)
Choose the correct completions.

1. Professor Wills is deeply involved   by / in   campus politics.

2. Who is qualified   for / in   this job?

3. Are you worried   for / about   your grade in this class?

4. A lot of people are interested   in / about   the astronauts in space.

5. Your last name is Mason? Are you related   with / to   Tony Mason?

6. Ann doesn't travel on planes. She's terrified   from / of   flying.

7. Mrs. Redmond? No, I'm not acquainted   to / with   her.

8. This is a wonderful book. I'll give it to you when I'm finished   with / for   it.

9. I'm bored   in / with   this movie. Can we leave?

10. Are you satisfied   for / with   our service? Let us know by email.

11. We are tired   from / of   paying rent, so we are going to buy an apartment.

12. Do you recycle? Are you committed   to / by   helping the environment?

PRACTICE 16 ▶ Passive vs. active. (Charts 11-1 → 11-6)
There is one verb error in each sentence. Correct the error.

1. The plane was arrived very late.

2. Four people injured in the accident.

3. Bella is married with José.

4. People are worried with global warming.

5. Astronomers are interesting in several new meteors.

6. We were surprise by Harold's announcement.

7. Spanish spoken by people in Mexico.

8. This road is not the right one. We lost.

9. Pat should try that new medicine. He might helped.

10. Lunch is been served in the cafeteria right now.

11. Something unusual was happened yesterday.

12. Will be fixed the refrigerator today?

PRACTICE 17 ▶ The passive with *get*. (Chart 11-7)
Complete the sentences with the words in the box.

chilly	dressed	hungry	invited	scared
crowded	elected	hurt	lost	stopped

1. At first, we were the only people in the restaurant, but it quickly got _____.

2. We can eat soon if you're getting _____.

3. Stan followed the map closely and didn't get _____.

4. When I heard those strange sounds last night, I got _____.

5. Wake up and get _____! We have to leave in five minutes.

6. Be careful on these old steps. You could fall and get _____.

7. Lola is disappointed because she didn't get _____ to the party.

8. Wear a jacket. You might get _____ tonight.

9. Don't drive so fast! You could get _____ for speeding!

10. Dr. Sousa is going to get _____ to the city government.

PRACTICE 18 ▸ Participial adjectives. (Chart 11-8)

Choose the correct completions.

1. a. When their team scored the winning point, the fans were   exciting / excited.

   b. The football game was very   exciting / excited.

2. a. The news I just heard was   shocking / shocked.

   b. Everyone was   shocking / shocked   by the news.

3. a. Our 40-mile bike ride was   exhausting / exhausted.

   b. I was   exhausting / exhausted   at the end of our bike ride.

4. a. This work is so   boring / bored.

   b. I'm very   boring / bored   with my work.

5. a. I'm really   confusing / confused.

   b. Professor Eng's explanation was   confusing / confused.

6. a. The ruins of the old city are very   interesting / interested.

   b. Archeologists are   interesting / interested   in the ruins of the old city.

7. a. The experience of climbing Mount Kilimanjaro was   thrilling / thrilled.

   b. The climber's family was   thrilling / thrilled   when she returned safely.

PRACTICE 19 ▸ -ed / -ing adjectives. (Chart 11-8)

Complete the sentences with the correct word from each pair.

1. *fascinating / fascinated*

   a. Your lecture was _____ .

   b. I was _____ by your lecture.

2. *exhausting / exhausted*

   a. Listening to Mrs. Wilson complain is _____ .

   b. I am _____ by Mrs. Wilson's complaints.

3. *disappointing / disappointed*

   a. Your parents are _____ in your behavior.

   b. Your behavior is _____ .

PRACTICE 20 ▸ -ed / -ing adjectives. (Chart 11-8)

Choose all the correct sentences in each group.

1. a. I am confused by these instructions.
   b. I am confusing by these instructions.
   c. These instructions are confused me.
   d. These instructions confuse me.

2. a. The history of civilization interests Professor Davis.
   b. The history of civilization is interesting to Professor Davis.
   c. The history of civilization is interested to Professor Davis.
   d. Professor Davis is interesting in the history of civilization.

3. a. I was embarrassing by all the attention.
   b. I was embarrassed by all the attention.
   c. All the attention embarrassed me.
   d. All the attention was embarrassed to me.

4. a. This is shocked news about your family.
   b. This is shocking news about your family.
   c. I was shocking by the news about your family.
   d. I was shocked by the news about your family.

5. a. Fred is boring by spectator sports.
   b. Spectator sports are boring to Fred.
   c. Fred is bored by spectator sports.
   d. Spectator sports are bored to Fred.

PRACTICE 21 ▶ -ed / -ing. (Chart 11-8)
Complete each sentence with the present or past participle of the verbs in parentheses.

1. There was an emergency on campus. We were not allowed to leave the buildings. The situation was

   very (*frustrate*) _____*frustrating*_____ .

2. As a little boy, Tom's jokes were cute, but as a (*grow*) _____ man, his jokes

   irritate people. Both Tom and his jokes are (*irritate*) _____ .

3. The invention of the (*wash*) _____ machine was a great help to households

   everywhere.

4. The pencil is a simple (*write*) _____ instrument.

5. We can eat (*freeze*) _____ yogurt after dinner.

6. This weather is (*depress*) _____ . I've been

   (*depress*) _____ all day.

7. You're going to laugh a lot when you see that movie. The critics say that it is the most

   (*entertain*) _____ movie of the year.

8. Here's a well-(*know*) _____ saying: "Don't cry over

   (*spill*) _____ milk." It means that you shouldn't worry about your past

   mistakes.

9. Here's a (*comfort*) _____ saying: "(*Bark*) _____

   dogs seldom bite." It means that some things may seem dangerous, but they often turn out not to

   be dangerous.

10. Here's an (*inspire*) _____ saying: "(*Unite*) _____

    we stand, (*divide*) _____ we fall." It means that we must stand together

    against an enemy in order to survive.

PRACTICE 22 ▸ Chapter review.
Choose the correct completions.

Termites are small wood-eating insects. Termites usually consider / are usually considered pests because they can do serious damage to unprotecting / unprotected buildings and other structures made about / of wood. In Zimbabwe termites build / are built enormous mounds. The termites grow a fungus inside the giant mounds. The fungus is the termites' primary food source. The fungus must be keeping / must be kept at exactly 87 degrees Fahrenheit, but temperatures in Zimbabwe can range / can be ranged from 35 to 104 degrees Fahrenheit. The termites build heating and cooling vents on their mounds. The temperature inside the mound regulates / is regulated as the termites constantly open and close the vents. In this way, the termites maintain / are maintained a constant temperature inside their mounds.

The Eastgate Centre in Harare, Zimbabwe is the country's largest shopping and office complex. Its architecture inspired / was inspired by termite mounds. The building has no air-conditioning system. Instead, it uses a ventilation system similar to the termite mounds. Air is drew / drawn into the building through the vents. The air warms or cools / is warmed or cooled by the mass of the concrete building.

The imitation of nature to solve complex human problems calls / is called biomimetics. The Eastgate Centre is an amazing / amazed example of biomimetics.

Appendix
Supplementary Grammar Units

PRACTICE 1 ▶ Subjects, verbs, and objects. (Chart A-1)
Underline and identify the subject (**S**), verb (**V**), and object of the verb (**O**) in each sentence.

        S   **V**   **O**
1. Airplanes have wings.
2. The teacher explained the problem.
3. Children enjoy games.
4. Jack wore a blue suit.
5. Some animals eat plants. Some animals eat other animals.
6. According to an experienced waitress, you can carry full cups of coffee without spilling them just by never looking at them.

PRACTICE 2 ▶ Transitive vs. intransitive verbs. (Chart A-1)
Underline and identify the verb in each sentence. Write **VT** if it is transitive. Write **VI** if it is intransitive.

          VI
1. Alice arrived at six o'clock.

          VT
2. We drank some tea.
3. I agree with you.
4. I waited for Sam at the airport for two hours.
5. They're staying at a resort hotel in San Antonio, Texas.
6. Mr. Chan is studying English.
7. The wind is blowing hard today.
8. I walked to the theater, but Janice rode her bicycle.
9. Crocodiles hatch from eggs.
10. Rivers flow toward the sea.

PRACTICE 3 ▶ Adjectives and adverbs. (Charts A-2 and A-3)
Underline and identify the adjectives (**ADJ**) and adverbs (**ADV**) in these sentences.

          ADJ   **ADV**
1. Jack opened the heavy door slowly.
2. Chinese jewelers carved beautiful ornaments from jade.
3. The old man carves wooden figures skillfully.
4. A busy executive usually has short conversations on the telephone.
5. The young woman had a very good time at the picnic yesterday.

PRACTICE 4 ▸ Adjectives and adverbs. (Charts A-2 and A-3)
Complete each sentence with the correct adjective or adverb.

1. *quick, quickly*   We ate ____quickly____ and ran to the theater.

2. *quick, quickly*   We had a ____quick____ dinner and ran to the theater.

3. *polite, politely*   I've always found Fred to be a _____ person.

4. *polite, politely*   He responded to my question _____.

5. *regular, regularly* Mr. Thomas comes to the store _____ for cheese and bread.

6. *regular, regularly* He is a _____ customer.

7. *usual, usually*   The teacher arrived at the _____ time.

8. *usual, usually*   She _____ comes to class five minutes before it begins.

9. *good, well*   Jennifer Cooper paints _____.

10. *good, well*   She is a _____ artist.

11. *gentle, gently*   A _____ breeze touched my face.

12. *gentle, gently*   A breeze _____ touched my face.

13. *bad, badly*   The audience booed the actors' _____ performance.

14. *bad, badly*   The audience booed and whistled because the actors performed

_____ throughout the show.

PRACTICE 5 ▸ Midsentence adverbs. (Chart A-3)
Put the adverb in parentheses in its usual midsentence position.

1. (*always*)   Ana ‸ takes a walk in the morning.
                        always

2. (*always*)   Tim is a hard worker.

3. (*always*)   Beth has worked hard.

4. (*always*)   Carrie works hard.

5. (*always*)   Do you work hard?

6. (*usually*)   Taxis are available at the airport.

7. (*rarely*)   Yusef takes a taxi to his office.

8. (*often*)   I have thought about quitting my job and sailing to Alaska.

9. (*probably*)   Yuko needs some help.

10. (*ever*)   Have you attended the show at the Museum of Space?

11. (*seldom*)   Brad goes out to eat at a restaurant.

12. (*hardly ever*) The students are late.

13. (*usually*)   Do you finish your homework before dinner?

14. (*generally*) In India, the monsoon season begins in April.

15. (*usually*)   During the monsoon season, Mr. Singh's hometown receives around 610 centimeters

(240 inches) of rain, which is an unusually large amount.

PRACTICE 6 ▸ Identifying prepositions. (Chart A-4)
Underline the prepositions.

1. Jim came to class <u>without</u> his books.

2. We stayed at home during the storm.

3. Sonya walked across the bridge over the Cedar River.

4. When Alex walked through the door, his little sister ran toward him and put her arms around his neck.

5. The two of us need to talk to Tom too.

6. Animals live in all parts of the world. Animals walk or crawl on land, fly in the air, and swim in the water.

7. Scientists divide living things into two main groups: the animal kingdom and the plant kingdom.

8. Asia extends from the Pacific Ocean in the east to Africa and Europe in the west.

PRACTICE 7 ▸ Sentence elements. (Charts A-1 → A-4)
Underline and identify the subject (**s**), verb (**v**), object (**o**), and prepositional phrases (**pp**) in the following sentences.

      S   **V**   **O**   **PP**
1. <u>Harry</u> <u>put</u> the <u>letter</u> <u>in the mailbox</u>.

2. The kids walked to school.

3. Caroline did her homework at the library.

4. Chinese printers created the first paper money in the world.

5. Dark clouds appeared on the horizon.

6. Rhonda filled the shelves of the cabinet with boxes of old books.

PRACTICE 8 ▸ Preposition combinations. (Chart A-5)
Choose <u>all</u> the correct completions for each sentence.

1. Max is known for his (*honesty* / *fairness* / *famous*).

2. Several students were absent from (*yesterday* / *school* / *class*).

3. Has Maya recovered from (*her illness* / *her husband's death* / *the chair*)?

4. The criminal escaped from (*jail* / *the key* / *prison*).

5. Do you believe in (*ghosts* / *UFOs* / *scary*)?

6. Anthony is engaged to (*my cousin* / *a friend* / *marriage*).

7. Chris excels in (*mathematics* / *sports* / *his cousins*).

8. I'm very fond of (*you* / *exciting* / *your children*).

9. Henry doesn't approve of (*smoking* / *cigarettes* / *rain*).

10. I subscribe to (*magazines* / *a newspaper* / *websites*).

PRACTICE 9 ▸ Preposition combinations. (Chart A-5)
Choose the correct prepositions in parentheses.

1. Water consists (*of* / *with*) oxygen and hydrogen.

2. I am uncomfortable because that man is staring (*to* / *at*) me.

3. Ella hid the candy (*from* / *back*) the children.

4. I arrived (*in / to*) this country two weeks ago.

5. We arrived (*to / at*) the airport ten minutes late.

6. I am envious (*in / of*) people who can speak three or four languages fluently.

7. The students responded (*at / to*) the teacher's questions.

8. The farmers are hoping (*on / for*) rain.

9. I'm depending (*on / in*) you to finish this work for me.

10. Tim wore sunglasses to protect his eyes (*for / from*) the sun.

PRACTICE 10 ▸ Preposition combinations. (Chart A-5)
Complete the sentences with appropriate prepositions.

SITUATION 1: Mr. and Mrs. Jones just celebrated their 50th wedding anniversary.

1. They have been married _____ *to* _____ each other for 50 years.

2. They have always been faithful _____ each other.

3. They are proud _____ their marriage.

4. They are polite _____ one another.

5. They are patient _____ each other.

6. They are devoted _____ one another.

7. They have been committed _____ their marriage.

SITUATION 2: Jacob and Emily have been together for five months. They don't have a healthy relationship, and it probably won't last long.

1. They are often annoyed _____ each other's behavior.

2. They argue _____ each other every day.

3. They are bored _____ their relationship.

4. They are tired _____ one another.

5. Jacob is jealous _____ Emily's friends.

6. Emily is sometimes frightened _____ Jacob's moods.

PRACTICE 11 ▸ Preposition combinations. (Chart A-5)
Complete each sentence in Column A with the correct phrase from Column B.

Column A

1. My boots are made __*c*__ .

2. We hope you succeed _____ .

3. She forgave him _____ .

4. I'm going to take care _____ .

5. The firefighters rescued many people _____ .

6. I pray _____ .

7. Trucks are prohibited _____ .

Column B

a. from the burning building

b. for telling a lie

✓ c. of leather

d. from entering the tunnel

e. in winning the scholarship

f. of the children tonight

g. for peace

PRACTICE 12 ▸ Preposition combinations. (Chart A-5)
Complete the sentences with appropriate prepositions.

1. Andrea contributed her ideas _____*to*_____ the discussion.
2. Ms. Kleeman substituted _____ our regular teacher.
3. I can't distinguish one twin _____ the other.
4. Children rely _____ their parents for food and shelter.
5. I'm worried _____ this problem.
6. I don't care _____ spaghetti. I'd rather eat something else.
7. Charles doesn't seem to care _____ his bad grades.
8. I'm afraid I don't agree _____ you.
9. We decided _____ eight o'clock as the time we should meet.
10. I am not familiar _____ that author's works.
11. Do you promise to come? I'm counting _____ you to be here.
12. The little girl is afraid _____ an imaginary bear that lives in her closet.

PRACTICE 13 ▸ Preposition combinations. (Chart A-5)
Complete the sentences with appropriate prepositions.

1. We will fight _____*for*_____ our rights.
2. Who did you vote _____ in the last election?
3. Jason was late because he wasn't aware _____ the time.
4. I am grateful _____ you _____ your assistance.
5. Elena is not content _____ the progress she is making.
6. Paul's comments were not relevant _____ the topic under discussion.
7. Have you decided _____ a date for your wedding yet?
8. Patricia applied _____ admission _____ the university.
9. Daniel dreamed _____ some of his childhood friends last night.
10. Mr. Miyagi dreams _____ owning his own business someday.
11. The accused woman was innocent _____ the crime with which she was charged.
12. Ms. Sanders is friendly _____ everyone.
13. The secretary provided me _____ a great deal of information.
14. Ivan compared the wedding customs in his country _____ those in the United States.

PRACTICE 14 ▶ Review: basic question forms. (Chart B-1)

From the underlined sentences, make questions for the given answers. Fill in the blank spaces with the appropriate words. If no word is needed, write Ø.

1. *Chris can live there.*

	Question word	Auxiliary verb	Subject	Main verb	Rest of question	→	Answer
1a.	Ø	Can	Chris	live	there ?	→	Yes.
1b.	Where	can	Chris	live	Ø ?	→	There.
1c.	Who	can	Ø	live	there ?	→	Chris.

2. *Ron is living there.*

	Question word	Auxiliary verb	Subject	Main verb	Rest of question	→	Answer
2a.	Ø				there ?	→	Yes.
2b.	Where				Ø ?	→	There.
2c.	Who				there ?	→	Ron.

3. *Kate lives there.*

	Question word	Auxiliary verb	Subject	Main verb	Rest of question	→	Answer
3a.	Ø				there ?	→	Yes.
3b.	Where				Ø ?	→	There.
3c.	Who				there ?	→	Kate.

4. *Anna will live there.*

	Question word	Auxiliary verb	Subject	Main verb	Rest of question	→	Answer
4a.	Ø				there ?	→	Yes.
4b.	Where				Ø ?	→	There.
4c.	Who				there ?	→	Anna.

5. *Jack lived there.*

	Question word	Auxiliary verb	Subject	Main verb	Rest of question	→	Answer
5a.					there ?	→	Yes.
5b.					Ø ?	→	There.
5c.					there ?	→	Jack.

6. *Mary has lived there.*

	Question word	Auxiliary verb	Subject	Main verb	Rest of question	→	Answer
6a.					?	→	Yes.
6b.					?	→	There.
6c.					?	→	Mary.

PRACTICE 15 ▸ Yes / no and information questions. (Charts B-1 and B-2)

Make questions to fit the conversations. Notice in the examples that there is a short answer and then in parentheses a long answer. Your questions should produce those answers.

1. A: _____*When are you going to the zoo?*_____

   B: Tomorrow. (*I'm going to the zoo tomorrow.*)

2. A: _____*Are you going downtown later today?*_____

   B: Yes. (*I'm going downtown later today.*)

3. A: _____

   B: Yes. (*I live in an apartment.*)

4. A: _____

   B: In a condominium. (*Alex lives in a condominium.*)

5. A: _____

   B: Janice. (*Janice lives in that house.*)

6. A: _____

   B: Yes. (*I can speak French.*)

7. A: _____

   B: Jeff. (*Jeff can speak Arabic.*)

8. A: _____

   B: Two weeks ago. (*Ben arrived two weeks ago.*)

9. A: _____

   B: Mazzen. (*Mazzen arrived late.*)

10. A: _____

    B: The window. (*Ann is opening the window.*)

11. A: _____

    B: Opening the window. (*Ann is opening the window.*)

12. A: _____

    B: Her book. (*Mary opened her book.*)

13. A: _____

    B: Ramzy. (*Ramzy opened the door.*)

14. A: _____

    B: Yes. (*The mail has arrived.*)

15. A: _____

    B: Yes. (*I have a bicycle.*)

16. A: _____

    B: A pen. (*Zach has a pen in his hand.*)

17. A: _____

    B: Yes. (*I like ice cream.*)

18. A: _____

    B: Yes. (*I would like an ice cream cone.*)

19. A: _____

    B: A candy bar. (*Scott would like a candy bar.*)

20. A: _____

    B: Isabel. (*Isabel would like a soft drink.*)

PRACTICE 16 ▶ Information questions. (Charts B-1 and B-2)

Make questions from these sentences. The *italicized* words in parentheses should be the answers to your questions.

1. I take my coffee (*black*). → *How do you take your coffee?*

2. I have (*an English-Spanish*) dictionary.

3. He (*runs a grocery store*) for a living.

4. Margaret was talking to (*her uncle*).

5. (*Only ten*) people showed up for the meeting.

6. (*Because of heavy fog*), none of the planes could take off.

7. She was thinking about (*her experiences as a rural doctor*).

8. I was driving (*sixty-five miles per hour*) when the police officer stopped me.

9. I like (*hot and spicy Mexican*) food best.

10. (*The*) apartment (*at the end of the hall on the second floor*) is mine.

11. Oscar is (*friendly, generous, and kindhearted*).

12. Oscar is (*tall and thin and has short black hair*).

13. (*Taylor's*) dictionary fell to the floor.

14. Abby isn't here (*because she has a doctor's appointment*).

15. All of the students in the class will be informed of their final grades (*on Friday*).

16. I feel (*awful*).

17. Of those three books, I preferred (*the one by Tolstoy*).

18. I like (*rock*) music.

19. The plane is expected to be (*an hour*) late.

20. The driver of the stalled car lit a flare (*in order to warn oncoming cars*).

21. I want (*the felt-tip*) pen, (*not the ballpoint*).

22. The weather is (*hot and humid*) in July.

23. I like my steak (*medium rare*).

24. I did (*very well*) on the test.

25. There are (*31,536,000*) seconds in a year.

PRACTICE 17 ▸ Information questions. (Charts B-1 and B-2)

Make questions from the following sentences. The words in parentheses should be the answers to your questions.

1. I need (*five dollars*). → *How much money do you need?*
2. Roberto was born (*in Panama*).
3. I go out to eat (*at least once a week*).
4. I'm waiting for (*Maria*).
5. (*My sister*) answered the phone.
6. I called (*Benjamin*).
7. (*Benjamin*) called.
8. She bought (*twelve gallons of*) gas.
9. "Deceitful" means (*"dishonest"*).
10. An abyss is (*a bottomless hole*).
11. He went (*this*) way, (*not that way*).
12. These are (*Scott's*) books and papers.
13. They have (*four*) children.
14. He has been here (*for two hours*).
15. It is (*two hundred miles*) to Madrid.
16. The doctor can see you (*at three on Friday*).
17. Her roommate is (*Jane Peters*).
18. Her roommates are (*Jane Peters and Ellen Lee*).
19. My parents have been living there (*for three years*).
20. This is (*Alice's*) book.
21. (*David and George*) are coming over for dinner.
22. Caroline's dress is (*blue*).
23. Caroline's eyes are (*brown*).
24. (*Andrew*) can't go on the picnic.
25. Andrew can't go (*because he is sick*).
26. I didn't answer the phone (*because I didn't hear it ring*).
27. I like (*classical*) music.
28. I don't understand (*the chart on page 50*).
29. Janie is (*studying*) right now.
30. You spell "sitting" (*with two "t's"—S-I-T-T-I-N-G*).
31. Xavier (*is about medium height and has red hair and freckles*).
32. Xavier is (*very serious and hard-working*).
33. Ray (*works as a civil engineer for the railroad company*).
34. Mexico is (*eight hundred miles*) from here.
35. I take my coffee (*black with sugar*).
36. Of Stockholm and Moscow, (*Stockholm*) is farther north.
37. (*Fine.*) I'm getting along (*just fine*).

PRACTICE 18 ▸ Shortened Yes/No Questions. (Chart B-3)
Make full questions from the shortened questions.

1. Find your keys? → *Did you find your keys?*

2. Want some coffee?

3. Need help?

4. Leaving already?

5. Have any questions?

6. (On an elevator) Going up?

7. Make it on time?

PRACTICE 19 ▸ Negative questions. (Chart B-4)
In these dialogues, make negative questions from the words in parentheses, and determine the expected response.

1. A: Your infected finger looks terrible. (*you, see, not*) ____*Haven't you seen*____ a doctor yet?
   B: ___*No*___. But I'm going to. I don't want the infection to get any worse.

2. A: You look pale. What's the matter? (*you, feel*) _____ well?
   B: _____. I think I might be coming down with something.

3. A: Did you see Mark at the meeting?
   B: No, I didn't.
   A: Really? (*he, be, not*) _____ there?
   B: _____.
   A: That's funny. I've never known him to miss a meeting before.

4. A: Why didn't you come to the meeting yesterday afternoon?
   B: What meeting? I didn't know there was a meeting.
   A: (*Dana, tell, not*) _____ you about it?
   B: _____. No one said a word to me about it.

5. A: I have a package for Jill. (*Jill and you, work, not*) _____
   _____ in the same building?
   B: _____. I'd be happy to take the package to her tomorrow when I go to work.

6. A: Kevin didn't report all of his income on his tax forms.
   B: (*that, be, not*) _____ against the law?
   A: _____. And that's why he's in a lot of legal trouble. He might even go to jail.

7. A: Did you give Miranda my message when you went to class this morning?
   B: No. I didn't see her.
   A: Oh? (*she, be*) _____ in class?
   B: _____. She didn't come today.

8. A: Do you see that woman over there, the one in the blue dress? (*she, be*) _____
   Mrs. Robbins?
   B: _____.
   A: I thought so. I wonder what she is doing here.

PRACTICE 20 ▶ Tag questions. (Chart B-5)

Add tag questions to the following.

1. You live in an apartment, _don't you_ ?

2. You've never been in Italy, _have you_ ?

3. Sara turned in her report, _____ ?

4. There are more countries north of the equator than south of it, _____ ?

5. You've never met Jack Freeman, _____ ?

6. You have a ticket to the game, _____ ?

7. You'll be there, _____ ?

8. John knows Claire Reed, _____ ?

9. We should call Rhonda, _____ ?

10. Ostriches can't swim, _____ ?

11. These books aren't yours, _____ ?

12. That's Charlie's, _____ ?

13. Your neighbors died in the accident, _____ ?

14. I'm right, _____ ?

15. This grammar is easy, _____ ?

PRACTICE 21 ▶ Contractions. (Chart C)

Write the contraction of the pronoun and verb if appropriate. Write Ø if the pronoun and verb cannot be contracted.

1. He is (_He's_) in my class.

2. He was (_Ø_) in my class.

3. He has (_He's_) been here since July.

4. He has (_Ø_) a Volvo.★

5. She had (_____) been there for a long time before we arrived.

6. She had (_____) a bad cold.

7. She would (_____) like to go to the zoo.

8. I did (_____) well on the test.

9. We will (_____) be there early.

10. They are (_____) in their seats over there.

11. It is (_____) going to be hot tomorrow.

12. It has (_____) been a long time since I've seen him.

13. A bear is a large animal. It has (_____) four legs and brown hair.★

14. We were (_____) on time.

15. We are (_____) always on time.

16. She has (_____) a good job.★

17. She has (_____) been working there for a long time.

★NOTE: *has, have,* and *had* are NOT contracted when they are used as main verbs. They are contracted only when they are used as helping verbs.

18. She had (_____) opened the window before class began.

19. She would (_____) have helped us if we had (_____) asked her.

20. He could have helped us if he had (_____) been there.

PRACTICE 22 ▸ Using *not* and *no*. (Chart D-1)

Change each sentence into the negative in two ways: use *not . . . any* in one sentence and *no* in the other.

1. I have some problems. → *I don't have any problems. I have no problems.*

2. There was some food on the shelf.

3. I received some letters from home.

4. I need some help.

5. We have some time to waste.

6. You should have given the beggar some money.

7. I trust someone. → *I don't trust anyone. I trust no one.*★★

8. I saw someone.

9. There was someone in his room.

10. She can find somebody who knows about it.

PRACTICE 23 ▸ Avoiding double negatives. (Chart D-2)

Correct the errors in these sentences, all of which contain double negatives.

1. We don't have no time to waste.

   → *We have no time to waste.* OR *We don't have any time to waste.*

2. I didn't have no problems.

3. I can't do nothing about it.

4. You can't hardly ever understand her when she speaks.

5. I don't know neither Joy nor her husband.

6. Don't never drink water from that river without boiling it first.

7. Because I had to sit in the back row of the auditorium, I couldn't barely hear the speaker.

PRACTICE 24 ▸ Beginning a sentence with a negative word. (Chart D-3)

Change each sentence so that it begins with a negative word.

1. I had hardly stepped out of bed when the phone rang.

   → *Hardly had I stepped out of bed when the phone rang.*

2. I will never say that again.

3. I have scarcely ever enjoyed myself more than I did yesterday.

4. She rarely makes a mistake.

5. I will never trust him again because he lied to me.

6. It is hardly ever possible to get an appointment to see him.

7. I seldom skip breakfast.

8. I have never known a more generous person than Samantha.

★***They're, their,*** and ***there*** all have the same pronunciation.

★★Also spelled with a hyphen in British English: *no-one*

PRACTICE 25 ▸ Spelling of -ing forms. (Chart E-2)
Write the -ing form of each verb in the correct column.

	Just add -ing to the simple form.	**Drop the final -e and add -ing.**	**Double the final letter and add -ing.**
1. arrive		arriving	
2. copy	copying		
3. cut			cutting
4. enjoy			
5. fill			
6. happen			
7. hope			
8. leave			
9. make			
10. rub			
11. stay			
12. stop			
13. take			
14. win			
15. work			

PRACTICE 26 ▸ Spelling of -ed forms. (Chart E-2)
Write the -ed form for each verb in the correct column.

	Just add -ed to the simple form.	**Add -d only.**	**Double the final letter and add -ed.**	**Change the -y to -i and add -ed.**
1. bother	bothered			
2. copy				copied
3. enjoy				
4. snore				
5. fear				
6. occur				
7. pat				
8. play				
9. rain				
10. refer				
11. reply				
12. return				
13. scare				
14. try				
15. walk				

PRACTICE 27 ▸ The simple tenses and the progressive tenses. (Chart E-3)
Circle the correct verb to complete each sentence.

1. It (*is raining* / *rains*) every day in August.

2. Uncle Joe (*visited* / *visits*) us last month.

3. Our team (*will win* / *wins*) the soccer game tomorrow.

4. Nick (*watches* / *is watching*) an action movie on TV now.

5. Tomorrow at this time we (*will be flying* / *are flying*) over the Atlantic Ocean.

6. Tina! I (*was thinking* / *am thinking*) of you just a minute ago when the phone rang!

7. I know you, Aunt Martha. You're never going to retire. You (*are working* / *will be working*) at your computer even when you are 90 years old.

8. At 9:00 P.M. last night, all the children (*go* / *went*) to bed. At 10:00 P.M. they (*slept* / *were sleeping*).

9. Uh-oh. Look! Mr. Anton (*fell* / *was falling*) down on the ice. Mr. Anton! Don't move! We (*help* / *will help*) you!

10. A: Why is the beach closed today?

    B: There are sharks in the water! They (*swim* / *are swimming*) near the shore!

PRACTICE 28 ▸ The perfect tenses. (Chart E-3)
Circle the correct verb to complete each sentence.

1. I (*have* / *had*) already seen the movie twice.

2. I (*have* / *had*) already seen the movie, so I didn't want to see it again.

3. Matthew (*has been* / *was*) a professor at this university since 2001. He's going to be chairman of the English department next year.

4. Fred (*has been* / *was*) a judge in the Supreme Court of this state for 21 years until he retired last year.

5. On the 14th of next month, my grandparents are going to celebrate their 50th wedding anniversary. They (*will have been* / *had been*) married for 50 years.

6. Rafael and Julie live in Springfield. They (*lived* / *have lived*) there all their lives.

7. Susanna and Jeff moved to Chicago. Before that, they (*have* / *had*) lived in this town all their lives.

8. Sorry, Mr. Wu. You (*have* / *will have*) missed your flight! The plane left just two minutes ago.

9. Javier speaks excellent English. He (*had* / *has*) studied English in school for twelve years before he came here.

10. We were too late to have dinner at the restaurant. When we got there, it (*has* / *had*) already closed for the night.

PRACTICE 29 ▸ The perfect progressive tenses. (Chart E-3)
Circle the correct verb to complete each sentence.

1. I'm thirsty, aren't you? We (*have* / *had*) been driving for four hours. Let's stop for a cold drink soon.

2. When is the rain going to stop? It (*has been* / *was*) raining for two days.

3. When Greta graduates from medical school next year, she (*will be / will have been*) studying for twenty years!

4. After Jim and Kim (*have / had*) been going out together for seven years, they finally got married last month.

5. You (*has / have*) been working in this office for only two months, and you've already gotten a raise? That's great!

6. Stan finally quit playing professional tennis after he broke his ankle two months ago. He (*has / had*) been playing for twenty years.

7. Well, it's good to be on this plane. Finally! We (*have been waiting / will have been waiting*) almost two hours!

8. Wake Maria up now. She (*had / has*) been sleeping for three hours. That's a very long nap.

9. The police officer gave Pedro a ticket because he (*has / had*) been speeding.

PRACTICE 30 ▸ Summary of verb tenses. (Charts E-4)
Write the correct form of the verbs in parentheses to complete the sentences.

	SIMPLE	PROGRESSIVE
PRESENT	1. Tom has regular habits. He (*eat*) _____ dinner every day. He has eaten dinner every day since he was a child. He ate dinner every day last month. He ate dinner yesterday. He will eat dinner tomorrow. He will probably eat dinner almost every day until the end of his life.	4. At 7:00 this evening, Tom started to eat dinner. It is now 7:15. Tom is on the phone because Mary called him. He says, "Can I call you back? I (*eat*) _____ dinner right now. I'll finish soon and will call you back. I don't want my dinner to get cold." Tom's dinner is in progress when Mary calls.
PAST	2. Tom eats dinner every day. Usually he eats at home, but yesterday, he (*eat*) _____ dinner at a restaurant.	5. Last week Tom went to a restaurant. He began to eat at 7:00. At 7:15 Mary came into the restaurant, saw Tom, and walked over to say hello. Tom's dinner was still in front of him. He hadn't finished it yet. In other words, when Mary walked into the restaurant, Tom (*eat*) _____ dinner. Tom's dinner was in progress when Mary arrived.
FUTURE	3. Tom ate dinner yesterday. He eats dinner every day. In all probability, he (*eat*) _____ dinner tomorrow.	6. Tom will begin his dinner at 7:00 tonight. Mary will arrive at 7:15. It takes Tom 30 minutes to eat his dinner. In other words, when Mary arrives tonight, Tom (*eat*) _____ his dinner. Tom's dinner will be in progress when Mary arrives.

	PERFECT	PERFECT PROGRESSIVE
PRESENT	7. Tom finished eating dinner at 7:30 tonight. It is now 8:00, and his mother has just come into the kitchen. She says, "What would you like for dinner? Can I cook something for you?" Tom says, "Thanks Mom, but I (*eat, already*) _____ dinner."	10. Tom began to eat dinner at 7:00 tonight. It is now, at this moment, 7:15. Tom (*eat*) _____ _____ his dinner for 15 minutes, but he hasn't finished yet. In other words, his dinner has been in progress for 15 minutes.
PAST	8. Yesterday Tom cooked his own dinner. He began at 7:00 and finished at 7:30. At 8:00 his mother came into the kitchen. She offered to cook some food for Tom, but he (*eat, already*) _____ . In other words, Tom had finished his dinner before he talked to his mother.	11. Last week Tom went to a restaurant. He began to eat at 7:00. At 7:15 Mary came into the restaurant, saw Tom, and walked over to say hello. Tom's dinner was still in front of him. He hadn't finished it yet. In other words, when Mary walked into the restaurant, Tom (*eat*) _____ dinner. Tom's dinner was in progress when Mary arrived.
FUTURE	9. Tomorrow Tom will begin dinner at 7:00 and finish at 7:30. His mother will come into the kitchen at 8:00. In other words, Tom (*eat, already*) _____ dinner by the time his mother walks into the kitchen.	12. Tonight Tom will go to a restaurant. He will begin to eat at 7:00. At 7:15 Mary will come into the restaurant, see Tom, and walk over to say hello. Tom's dinner will still be in front of him. He won't have finished it yet. In other words, when Mary walks into the restaurant, Tom (*eat*) _____ _____ dinner for 15 minutes. Tom's dinner will have been in progress for 15 minutes by the time Mary arrives.

PRACTICE 31 ▸ Linking verbs. (Chart E-7)

Some of the *italicized* words in the following are used as linking verbs. Identify which ones are linking verbs by underlining them. Also underline the adjective that follows the linking verb.

1. Olivia *looked* at the fruit. (*no underline*)

2. It *looked* fresh.

3. Dan *noticed* a scratch on the door of his car.

4. Morris *tasted* the candy.

5. It *tasted* good.

6. The crowd *grew* quiet as the official began her speech.

7. Felix *grows* tomatoes in his garden.

8. Bella *grew* up in Florida.

9. I can *smell* the chicken in the oven.

10. It *smells* delicious.

11. Dahlia *got* a package in the mail.

12. Allie *got* sleepy after dinner.

13. During the storm, the sea *became* rough.

14. Vanessa *became* a doctor after many years of study.

15. Diana *sounded* her horn to warn the driver of the other car.

16. Helen *sounded* happy when I talked to her.

17. The weather *turns* hot in July.

18. When Aiden entered the room, I *turned* around to look at him.

19. I *turned* a page in the book.

20. It *appears* certain that Mary Hanson will win the election.

21. Cameron's story *seems* strange. Do you believe it?

PRACTICE 32 ▶ Linking verbs; adjectives and adverbs. (Chart E-7)
Complete each sentence with the correct adjective or adverb.

1. *clean, cleanly*   The floor looks _____*clean*_____.

2. *slow, slowly*   The bear climbed _____*slowly*_____ up the tree.

3. *safe, safely*   The plane landed _____ on the runway.

4. *anxious, anxiously*   When the wind started to blow, I grew _____.

5. *complete, completely* This list of names appears _____. No more names need to be added.

6. *wild, wildly*   The crowd yelled _____ when we scored a goal.

7. *honest, honestly*   The clerk looked _____, but she wasn't. I discovered when I got home that she had cheated me.

8. *thoughtful, thoughtfully* Jane looked at her book _____ before she answered the teacher's question.

9. *good, well*   Most of the students did _____ on their tests.

10. *fair, fairly*   The contract offer sounded _____ to me, so I accepted the job.

11. *terrible, terribly* Jim felt _____ about forgetting his son's birthday.

12. *good, well*   A rose smells _____.

13. *light, lightly*   As dawn approached, the sky became _____.

14. *confident, confidently* Kennedy spoke _____ when she delivered her speech.

15. *famous, famously*   The actor became _____ throughout much of the world.

16. *fine, finely*   I don't think this milk is spoiled. It tastes _____ to me.

PRACTICE 33 ▶ Troublesome verbs. (Chart E-8)
Choose the correct verb in parentheses.

1. The student (*raised*/ *rose*) his hand in class.

2. Hot air (*raises / rises*).

3. Natasha (*set / sat*) in a chair because she was tired.

4. I (*set / sat*) your dictionary on the table a few minutes ago.

5. Hens (*lay / lie*) eggs.

6. Sara is (*laying / lying*) on the grass in the park right now.

7. Jan (*laid / lay*) the comb on top of the dresser a few minutes ago.

8. If you are tired, you should (*lay / lie*) down and take a nap.

9. San Francisco (*lays / lies*) to the north of Los Angeles.

10. Mr. Faust (*raises / rises*) many different kinds of flowers in his garden.

11. The student (*raised / rose*) from her seat and walked to the front of the auditorium to receive her diploma.

12. Hiroki is a very methodical person. Every night before going to bed, he (*lays / lies*) his clothes for the next day on his chair.

13. Where are my keys? I (*lay / laid*) them here on the desk five minutes ago.

14. Fahad (*set / sat*) the table for dinner.

15. Fahad (*set / sat*) at the table for dinner.

16. The fulfillment of all your dreams (*lies / lays*) within you — if you just believe in yourself.

Special Workbook Section

Phrasal Verbs

PHRASAL VERBS (TWO-WORD AND THREE-WORD VERBS)

The term *phrasal verb* refers to a verb and particle which together have a special meaning. For example, ***put + off*** means "postpone." Sometimes a phrasal verb consists of three parts. For example, ***put + up + with*** means "tolerate." Phrasal verbs are also called *two-word verbs* or *three-word verbs*.

SEPARABLE PHRASAL VERBS (a) ***I handed*** *my paper* ***in*** yesterday. (b) ***I handed in*** *my paper* yesterday. (c) ***I handed*** *it* ***in*** yesterday. (*INCORRECT:* I *handed in it* yesterday.)	A phrasal verb may be either *separable* or *nonseparable*. With a separable phrasal verb, a noun may come either between the verb and the preposition or after the preposition, as in (a) and (b). A pronoun comes between the verb and the preposition if the phrasal verb is separable, as in (c).

NONSEPARABLE PHRASAL VERBS
(d) ***I ran into*** *an old friend* yesterday.
(e) ***I ran into*** *her* yesterday.
    (*INCORRECT:* I *ran an old friend into.*)
    (*INCORRECT:* I *ran her into* yesterday.)
	With a nonseparable phrasal verb, a noun or pronoun must follow the preposition, as in (d) and (e).

Phrasal verbs are especially common in informal English. Following is a list of common phrasal verbs and their usual meanings. This list contains only those phrasal verbs used in the exercises in the text. The phrasal verbs marked with an asterisk (*) are nonseparable.

A   ask out . . . . *ask someone to go on a date*

B   bring about, bring on . . . . *cause*
         bring up . . . . *(1) rear children; (2) mention or introduce a topic*

C   call back . . . . *return a telephone call*
         call in . . . . *ask to come to an official place for a specific purpose*
         call off . . . . *cancel*
         *call on . . . . *ask to speak in class*
         call up . . . . *call on the telephone*
         *catch up (with) . . . . *reach the same position or level*
         *check in, check into . . . . *register at a hotel*
         check into . . . . *investigate*
         check out . . . . *(1) borrow a book from the library; (2) investigate*
         check out (of) . . . . *leave a hotel*
         cheer up . . . . *make (someone) feel happier*
         clean up . . . . *make clean and orderly*
         *come across . . . . *meet / find by chance*
         cross out . . . . *draw a line through*
         cut out . . . . *stop an annoying activity*

D   do over . . . . *do again*
         *drop by, drop in (on) . . . . *visit informally*
         drop off . . . . *leave something / someone at a place*
         *drop out (of) . . . . *stop going to school, to a class, to a club, etc.*

F   figure out . . . . *find the answer by reasoning*

        fill out. . . . . *write the answers to a questionnaire or complete an official form*

        find out . . . . *discover information*

G   *get along (with) . . . . *have a good relationship with*

        get back (from). . . . . *(1) return from a place; (2) receive again*

        *get in, get into. . . . . *(1) enter a car; (2) arrive*

        *get off. . . . . *leave an airplane, a bus, a train, a subway, a bicycle*

        *get on. . . . . *enter an airplane, a bus, a train, a subway, a bicycle*

        *get out of . . . . *(1) leave a car; (2) avoid work or an unpleasant activity*

        get over. . . . . *recover from an illness*

        get through (with). . . . . *finish*

        *get up (from) . . . . *arise from a bed, a chair*

        give back . . . . *return an item to someone*

        give up . . . . *stop trying, quit*

        *go over . . . . *review or check carefully*

        *grow up . . . . *become an adult*

H   hand in. . . . . *submit an assignment*

        hang up . . . . *(1) conclude a telephone conversation; (2) put clothes on a hanger or a hook*

        have on. . . . . *wear*

K   keep out (of) . . . . *not enter*

        *keep up (with) . . . . *stay at the same position or level*

        kick out (of). *force (someone) to leave*

L   *look after . . . . *take care of*

        *look into. . . . . *investigate*

        *look out (for) . . . . *be careful*

        look over. . . . . *review or check carefully*

        look up. . . . . *look for information in a reference book, on the internet, etc.*

M   make up . . . . *(1) invent; (2) do past-due work*

N   name after, name for. . . . . *give a baby the name of someone else*

P   *pass away, pass on. . . . . *die*

        pass out . . . . *distribute*

        *pass out . . . . *lose consciousness*

        pick out . . . . *select*

        pick up. . . . . *(1) go to get someone (e.g., in a car); (2) take in one's hand*

        point out . . . . *call attention to*

        put away. . . . . *remove to a proper place*

        put back. . . . . *return to the original place*

        put off . . . . *postpone*

        put on . . . . *put clothes on one's body*

        put out. . . . . *extinguish a cigarette, cigar, fire*

        *put up with. . . . . *tolerate*

R   *run into, *run across. . . . . *meet by chance*

        *run out (of) . . . . *finish a supply of something*

S   *show up . . . . *appear, come*

        shut off. . . . . *stop a machine, light, faucet*

T *take after . . . . *resemble*
take off. . . . . *(1) remove clothing; (2) leave on a trip*
take out . . . . *(1) take someone on a date; (2) remove*
take over. . . . . *take control*
take up . . . . *begin a new activity or topic*
tear down . . . . *demolish; reduce to nothing*
tear up . . . . *tear into many little pieces*
think over . . . . *consider carefully*
throw away, throw out. . . . . *discard, get rid of*
throw up. . . . . *vomit; regurgitate food*
try on . . . . *put on clothing to see if it fits*
turn down . . . . *decrease volume or intensity*
turn in . . . . *(1) submit an assignment; (2) go to bed*
turn off. . . . . *stop a machine, light, faucet*
turn on. . . . . *start a machine, light, faucet*
turn out . . . . *extinguish a light*
turn up. . . . . *increase volume or intensity*

PRACTICE 1 ▶ Phrasal verbs.

Complete each sentence with the appropriate preposition(s). The meaning of the phrasal verb is in parentheses.

1. Lara looked . . .

   a. ____after____ her father when he was sick. (*took care of*)

   b. _____ her children's homework. (*reviewed*)

   c. _____ some information on the Internet. (*looked for information*)

   d. _____ an unusual situation at work. (*investigated*)

2. The tourists checked . . .

   a. _____ travel DVDs from the library before their trip. (*borrowed*)

   b. _____ their hotel. (*registered at*)

   c. _____ a famous archeological site. (*investigated*)

   d. _____ _____ their hotel rooms. (*left*)

3. Mrs. Jenkins got . . .

   a. _____ a serious illness. (*recovered from*)

   b. _____ _____ her planning for her daughter's wedding. (*finished*)

   c. _____ _____ doing an unimportant project at work. (*avoided*)

   d. _____ _____ her summer vacation early. (*returned*)

   e. _____ the subway at an unfamiliar stop. (*left*)

4. The school principal called . . .

   a. _____ the school assembly. (*canceled*)

   b. _____ some parents. (*telephoned*)

   c. _____ a few students to answer questions while visiting a class. (*asked them to speak*)

   d. _____ a teacher who was sick. (*returned a phone call*)

   e. _____ a student for discipline. (*asked the student to come to his/her office*)

PRACTICE 2 ▸ Phrasal verbs.

Complete each sentence with the correct form of a phrasal verb from the list. One phrasal verb is used twice.

get along with	pass out (2)	put up with	take after	turn in
pass away	pick out	show up	think over	

1. The flight attendants gave one snack to passengers during the flight. They __passed__ __out__ small bags of peanuts.

2. You choose the vegetables for dinner. _____ _____ whatever you like.

3. You look like your mother, but your brother _____ _____ your father.

4. I have three good job offers to consider. I need some time to _____ them _____.

5. Nathan tolerates his roommate's messy habits. I wonder how he _____ _____ _____ them.

6. Mary's elderly mother died last week. She _____ _____ after a long illness.

7. Julianna was two hours late for the dinner party. When she finally appeared, her friends told her it was rude to _____ _____ so late.

8. The Smiths are a friendly couple and people really like them. They seem to _____ _____ _____ everyone.

9. Good night. It's bedtime. I'm going to _____ _____ now.

10. Hannah got hit in the head with a golf ball, but fortunately didn't lose consciousness. The ball was traveling so fast that it was a miracle she didn't _____ _____.

PRACTICE 3 ▸ Phrasal verbs.

Choose the correct completions. More than one completion may be correct.

1. When do we turn in   (our assignment?)   the dinner?   yesterday?
2. Mario made up   a lie.   a story.   a flower.
3. The government took over   the city.   the banks.   the trees.
4. Please put out   your cigarette.   the lights.   the fire.
5. What brought about   the war?   the package?   the crisis?
6. Did you figure out   working?   the problem?   the puzzle?
7. How do I turn on   the lights?   the music?   the printer?
8. Hugo asked out   his classmate.   a question.   a girl.
9. Jill is going to give up   a present.   chocolate.   smoking.
10. At the airport, I came across a friend.   a classmate.   to fly.
11. Tina dropped out of   high school.   the ball.   college.

PRACTICE 4 ▸ Phrasal verbs.

Complete each sentence with an appropriate preposition from the list to form a two-word verb. Some prepositions may be used more than once.

| back | into | off | on | out | up |

1. A: Guess who I ran ___*into*___ today as I was walking across campus. Ann Keefe!

   B: You're kidding!

2. A: There will be a test on Chapters 8 and 9 next Friday.

   B: Oh, no! Couldn't you put it _____ until Monday?

3. A: You'd better put _____ your coat before you leave. It's chilly out.

   B: What's the temperature?

4. A: I smell something burning in the kitchen. Can I call you

   _____ in a minute?

   B: Sure. I hope your dinner hasn't burned.

   A: So do I! Bye.

5. A: I think that if I learn enough vocabulary I won't have any

   trouble using English.

   B: That's not necessarily so. I'd like to point _____ that

   language consists of much more than just vocabulary.

6. A: Your children certainly love the outdoors.

   B: Yes, they do. We brought them _____ to appreciate nature.

7. A: What forms do I have to fill out to change my tourist visa to a student visa?

   B: I don't know, but I'll look _____ it first thing tomorrow and try to find

   _____. I'll let you know.

8. A: How long were you in the hospital?

   B: About a week. But I've missed almost two weeks of classes.

   A: It's going to be hard for you to make _____ all the work you've missed, isn't it?

   B: Very.

9. A: Could you pick _____ a newspaper on your way home from work tonight? There's a

   story I want to read.

   B: Sure.

10. A: I like your new shoes.

    B: Thanks. I had to try _____ almost a dozen pairs before I decided to get these.

PRACTICE 5 ▶ Phrasal verbs.

Complete each sentence with an appropriate preposition from the list to form a two-word verb. Some prepositions may be used more than once.

about	away	in	of	off	on	out	up

1. A: I'm trying to find yesterday's newspaper. Have you seen it?

   B: I'm afraid I threw it ___*away / out*___ . I thought you had finished reading it.

2. A: Where did you grow _____?

   B: In Seattle, Washington.

3. A: Don't forget to turn the lights _____ before you go to bed.

   B: I won't.

4. A: I have a car, so I can drive us to the festival.

   B: Good.

   A: What time should I pick you _____?

   B: Any time after five would be fine.

5. A: We couldn't see the show at the outdoor theater last night.

   B: Why not?

   A: It was called _____ on account of rain.

6. A: Thomas looks sad.

   B: I think he misses his girlfriend. Let's try to cheer him _____.

7. A: What brought _____ your decision to quit your present job?

   B: I was offered a better job.

8. A: Why did you come back early from your trip?

   B: Unfortunately, I ran _____ _____ money.

9. A: Thanks for the ride. I appreciate it.

   B: Where should I drop you _____?

10. A: What time does your plane take _____?

    B: 10:40.

    A: How long does the flight take?

    B: I think we get _____ around 12:30.

PRACTICE 6 ▶ Phrasal verbs.

Complete the sentences with appropriate prepositions to form two-word or three-word verbs.

1. A: Look ___*out*___! A car is coming!

2. A: May I borrow your dictionary?

   B: Sure. But please be sure to put it _____ on the shelf when you're finished.

3. A: I'm going to be in your neighborhood tomorrow.

   B: Oh? If you have time, why don't you drop _____ to see us?

4. A: How does this tape recorder work?

B: Push this button to turn it _____ and push that button to shut it _____.

5. A: Did you hear what started the forest fire?

B: Yes. Some campers built a fire, but when they left their campsite, they didn't _____ it _____ completely.

6. A: I need to talk to Karen.

B: Why don't you call her _____? She's probably at home now.

7. A: Uh-oh. I made a mistake on the check I just wrote.

B: Don't try to correct the mistake. Just tear _____ the check and throw it _____.

8. A: Are you here to apply for a job?

B: Yes.

A: Here is an application form. Fill it _____ and then give it _____ to me when you are finished.

9. A: Look. There's Mike.

B: Where?

A: At the other end of the block, walking toward the administration building. If we run, we can catch _____ with him.

10. A: Is your roommate here?

B: Yes. She decided to come to the party after all. Have you ever met her?

A: No, but I'd like to.

B: She's the one standing over there by the far window. She has a blue dress _____. Come on. I'll introduce you.

PRACTICE 7 ▸ Phrasal verbs.

Complete each sentence with an appropriate preposition.

1. A: What time did you get _____*up*_____ this morning?

B: I slept late. I didn't drag myself out of bed until after nine.

2. A: How did you do on your composition?

B: Not well. It had a lot of spelling mistakes, so I have to do it _____.

3. A: What's the baby's name?

B: Helen. She was named _____ her paternal grandmother.

4. A: I need to get more exercise.

B: Why don't you take _____ tennis?

5. A: You can't go in there.

   B: Why not?

   A: Look at that sign. It says, "Keep _____. No trespassing."

6. A: The radio is too loud. Would you mind if I turned it _____ a little?

   B: No.

7. A: I can't hear the radio. Could you turn it _____ a little?

   B: Sure.

8. A: What are you doing Saturday night, Bob?

   B: I'm taking Virginia _____ for dinner and a show.

9. A: Don't you think it's hot in here?

   B: Not especially. If you're hot, why don't you take your sweater _____?

10. A: How do you spell *occasionally*?

    B: I'm not sure. You'd better look it _____ in your dictionary.

11. A: I'm tired. I wish I could get _____ of going to the meeting tonight.

    B: Why do you have to go?

PRACTICE 8 ▸ Phrasal verbs.

Complete each sentence with an appropriate preposition.

1. A: I need my dictionary, but I lent it to José.

   B: Why don't you get it ___*back*___ from him?

2. A: Cindy is only three. She likes to play with the older kids, but when they're running and playing, she can't keep _____ with them.

   B: She doesn't seem to mind, does she?

3. A: I made a mistake in my composition. What should I do?

   B: Since it's an in-class composition, just cross it _____.

4. A: What happened when the pilot of the plane passed out during the flight?

   B: The co-pilot took _____.

5. I took a plane from Atlanta to Miami. I got _____ the plane in Atlanta. I got _____ the plane in Miami.

6. It was a snowy winter day, but I still had to drive to work. First I got _____ the car to start the engine. Then I got _____ of the car to scrape the snow and ice from the windows.

7. Last year I took a train trip. I got _____ the train in Chicago. I got _____ the train in Des Moines.

8. Jessica takes the bus to work. She gets _____ the bus at Lindbergh Boulevard and gets _____ the bus about two blocks from her office on Tower Street.

9. A: Do you like living in the dorm?

   B: It's OK. I've learned to put _____ _____ all the noise.

10. A: What brought _____ your decision to quit your job?

    B: I couldn't get _____ _____ my boss.

11. A: Did you go _____ your paper carefully before you handed it _____?

    B: Yes. I looked it _____ carefully.

Index

A/an, 64, 66–67
Able to, 79
Active verbs, 97–102, 104
Adjective(s):, 109–110
    with linking verbs (e.g., *taste good*), 125
    nouns used as (e.g., *vegetable soup*), 51–53
    participial (e.g., *amusing/amused*), 105–106
    passive verbs (stative) used as, 103
Adverb(s), 109–110
    with linking verbs, 125
    midsentence, 204
A few, 57–59
Ago, 16
Agreement:
    pronoun-noun, 70–71
    subject-verb, 43–49
A little, 58–59
A lot of, 57
Any, 120
Apostrophe, with possessive nouns, 53–55
Appositives (SEE Adjective phrases)
Articles, 63–68
As soon as, 28–29
Auxiliary verbs (SEE *Be; Do/does/did; Have/has/ had;* Modal auxiliaries; Questions)

Be, in passive form, 96–97
Be able to, 79
Be going to, 24–27, 97
Be supposed to, 78–79, 85–86

Can:
    degree of certainty in, 88
    in expressions of ability/possibility, 79–80, 86
    in polite requests, 80
Collective nouns, 44, 71
Contractions of verbs, 119–120
Could:
    degree of certainty in, 86–88
    in expressions of ability, 86
    in polite requests, 80
    progressive form of, 92
Count/noncount nouns, 55–58
    expressions of quantity with, 57–58

Definite nouns, 63–66
    articles with, 64
Do/does/did, in negatives, 120
Double negatives, 120

Each/every, 45, 60
Each of, 45, 60
-Ed forms, 4
    spelling of, 121
Every one of, 45, 60
Expressions of quantity, 45, 57–61, 126
        (SEE ALSO Past participle; Verb tenses,
        simple past)

(A) Few/(a) little, 57–59
For, vs. *since,* 15–16
Frequency adverbs, 110
Future time:
    expressing in time clauses, 28–29
    present tenses to express, 29–31
    (SEE ALSO *Be going to; Verb tenses; Will*)
    after verbs of perception, 145

Get, passive with (e.g., *get worried*), 104
Going to, 24–27

Had better, 77–78
Had to, 90
Have/has/had:
    contractions with, 17, 119–120, 119*fn.*
    in negative questions, 118
    in tag questions, 119
Have to:
    in expressions of necessity, 75–77
    past form of, 84
    in prohibitions, 76–77
How, 116
How much, 117
Hyphen, 120*fn.*

Impersonal pronouns, 72
Indefinite nouns, 63–66
    articles with, 64
Indefinite pronouns, 70–71

Information questions, 115–117
-Ing forms:
   in polite requests, 81
   spelling of, 121
Intransitive verbs, 109
Irregular plural nouns, 50–51
Irregular verbs, 4–7, 14, 125–126
Is, contractions with, 17
It, 70
   its vs. *it's,* 70

Know how to, 79

Let's, 82
Linking verbs, 124–125
(A) Little/(a) few, 57–59
-Ly, in adverbs, 109–110

Many/much, 57
May:
   degree of certainty in, 86–88
   in expressions of possibility, 80
   in polite requests, 80
   progressive form of, 92
Midsentence adverbs, 110
Might:
   degree of certainty in, 86–88
   in expressions of possibility, 80
   progressive form of, 92
Modal auxiliaries:
   passive form of, 102–103
   progressive forms of, 92
Most (of), 45
Much/many, 57
Must:
   degree of certainty in, 86–91
   in expressions of necessity, 75–77
   past form of, 84
   progressive form of, 92
   in prohibitions, 76–77

Negative(s), double, 120
Negative questions, 118
Negative sentences, 120
Negative words, 120
No, 120
Noncount nouns, 55–58
None (of), 45
Non-progressive verbs, 3, 103–104
No one, 120*fn.*
Not, 120
Noun(s):
   collective, 44, 71
   count and noncount, 55–58
   definite and indefinite, 63–66
   generic, 65, 70–71
   possessive (e.g., *John's book*), 53–55
   pronoun agreement with, 70–71
   regular and irregular plural, 50–51
   used as adjectives (e.g., *vegetable soup*), 51–53

Of, in expressions of quantity, 61
One:
   in expressions of quantity, 45, 60
   as impersonal pronoun, 72
One of (+ plural noun), 45, 60
Other:
   common expressions with, 74
   forms of, 72–73
Ought to, 77–78

Participial adjectives (e.g., *confusing* vs. *confused*),
   105–106
Participles (SEE Modifying phrases; Past participle,
   Present participle)
Passive (form), 96–102
   with *get* (e.g., *get worried*), 104
   modals and phrasal modals in, 102–103
   non-progressive (e.g., *the door is locked*),
      103–104
   participial adjectives in (e.g., *amused children*),
      105–106
Past participle, 4
   as adjective (e.g., *amused children*), 105–106
   irregular, 4
   vs. present participle, 105–106
Past time (SEE Verb tenses)
Perfect/perfect progressive verbs (SEE Verb tenses)
Personal pronouns, 69–71
   agreement with nouns, 70–71
Phrasal modals, 92
   passive form of, 102–103
Phrasal verbs, 127–135
Phrases:
   prepositional, 111
Polite requests, 80–82
Possessive nouns (e.g., *John's book*), 53–55
Preposition(s), 111
   in common combinations, 111–113
   after non-progressive passive verbs, 103–104
   in phrasal verbs, 129–135
Prepositional phrases, 111
Present participle:
   as adjective (e.g., *amusing story*), 105–106
   vs. past participle, 105–106
Present time (SEE Verb tenses)
Progressive verbs:
   modal auxiliaries as, 92
   vs. non-progressive, 3
   (SEE ALSO Verb tenses)
Pronouns:
   contractions with, 119–120
   impersonal, 72
   indefinite, 70–71

personal, 69–71
    agreement with nouns, 70–71
    reflexive, 71–72
Pronunciation, of *they're/their/there,* 120

Quantity (SEE Expressions of quantity)
Questions:
    basic forms of, 114
    information, 225–117
    negative, 118
    question words beginning, 114
    tag, 119
    word order in, 114
    yes/no, 115–116, 118

Reflexive pronouns, 71–72
Regular plural nouns, 50–51
Regular verbs, 4
Repeated action in the past (*would*), 83

-S/-es, 43–44, 51, 54–55
-Self/-selves, 71–72
Sentences:
    interrogative (SEE Questions)
    negative, 120
    simple (SEE Subjects, verbs, objects)
Shall, for suggestions, 82
Should:
    degree of certainty in, 91
    in expressions of advisability, 77–78
    in expressions of expectation, 79
    past form of, 84–85
    present form of, 85
    progressive form of, 92
Simple form of a verb:
    with irregular verbs, 14
Simple tenses (SEE Verb tenses)
Since:
    vs. *for,* 15–16
    for duration of time, 15–16
Singular/plural (SEE Agreement; Count/noncount
    nouns; Irregular plural nouns; Nouns, used
    as adjectives; *-s/-es*)
Some, 57–58, 63–64
Spelling:
    -ed/-ing, 121
    -s/-es, 44
Stative verbs (SEE Non-progressive verbs)
Subjects, verbs, objects, 109, 111
Subject-verb agreement, 43–49
Supposed to, 78–79, 85–86

Tag questions, 119
Tenses (SEE Verb tenses)
The, 64, 66–68
Their, 120*fn.*
There:
    + *be,* 45
    pronunciation of, 120*fn.*
They, as impersonal pronoun, 72
They're, 120*fn.*
Time clauses:
    expressing future in, 28–29
Transitive verbs, 109

Uncountable nouns (SEE Noncount nouns)
Used to, 83

Verb tenses:
    future perfect, 32
    future perfect progressive, 32
    future progressive, 31–32
    non-progressive, 3, 103–104
    in passive, 96–97
    past perfect, 20, 21–22
    past perfect progressive, 22–23
    past progressive, 7–9
    present perfect, 14–20
    present perfect progressive, 19–20, 22–23
    present progressive, 1–3, 29–31
    review of, 35–42, 122–124
    simple future, 24–25
    simple past, 6–9, 18, 20, 21–22
    simple present, 1–2, 29–30

When, 115
Where, 114
Who/whom, 114
Why don't, 82
Will:
    future, 25–27
Would:
    in polite requests, 80–82
    for repeated action in the past, 83
Would rather, 93
Would you mind, 81–82

Yes/no questions, 115–116, 118
You, as impersonal pronoun, 72

Answer Key

CHAPTER 1: PRESENT AND PAST; SIMPLE AND PROGRESSIVE

PRACTICE 1, p. 1

Many people <u>keep</u> indoor house plants for their natural beauty, but these plants also <u>create</u> a healthier living space. While scientists at NASA (National Aeronautics and Space Administration) <u>were researching</u> air quality in space stations, they <u>discovered</u> that common indoor house plants actually <u>clean</u> the air. The plants <u>absorb</u> carbon dioxide and <u>release</u> oxygen. NASA scientists <u>found</u> that plants also <u>eliminate</u> harmful chemicals in the air. In 1989, NASA <u>published</u> the first results of the NASA Clean Air Study. Today, scientists <u>are still learning</u> about the many benefits of houseplants.

1. keep, create, clean, absorb, release, eliminate
2. discovered, found, published
3. are learning
4. were researching

PRACTICE 2, p. 1

1. a. sets
   b. is setting
2. a. is raining / 's raining
   b. rains
3. a. listen
   b. am listening / 'm listening
4. a. form
   b. is forming
5. a. melts
   b. is melting

PRACTICE 3, p. 2

1. a. fall
   b. are falling
2. a. grows
   b. are growing
3. a. shines
   b. is shining ... are singing
4. a. beats
   b. is beating
5. a. sleep
   b. is sleeping

PRACTICE 4, p. 2

1. Does
2. Is
3. Do
4. Is
5. Does
6. Do
7. Are

PRACTICE 5, p. 2

1. doesn't rise
2. is revolving
3. live
4. is raining / isn't raining
5. freezes
6. make / don't make
7. are making / aren't making

PRACTICE 6, p. 3

1. a	6. a
2. b	7. b
3. a	8. a
4. b	9. a
5. a	10. a

PRACTICE 7, p. 3

1. a	4. a
2. b	5. b
3. b	6. a

PRACTICE 8, p. 4

Part I.
changed ... launched ... was ... weighed ... took ... ushered ... was ... marked

Part II.

1. T	4. F
2. F	5. T
3. T	

PRACTICE 9, p. 4

Part I.	**Part II.**
1. rained	1. hit
2. snowed	2. woke
3. listened	3. rose
	4. set

PRACTICE 10, p. 4

1. ran	9. went
2. drank	10. bought
3. swam	11. cost
4. won	12. ate
5. lost	13. gave
6. took	14. made
7. began	15. felt
8. taught	

PRACTICE 11, p. 5

1. sold
2. bought
3. began
4. had
5. caught
6. quit
7. found
8. made
9. took
10. broke
11. came
12. lost
13. slept
14. built
15. fought
16. understood
17. spent
18. let
19. saw
20. taught
21. spoke
22. went
23. paid
24. forgot
25. wrote
26. fell
27. felt
28. left
29. upset
30. flew

PRACTICE 12, p. 5

1. broke
2. stole
3. knew
4. heard
5. came
6. shook
7. hid
8. found
9. fought
10. ran
11. shot
12. caught

PRACTICE 13, p. 6

1. bit
2. held
3. meant
4. blew
5. quit
6. felt
7. stung
8. swam
9. paid
10. caught

PRACTICE 14, p. 7

1. spent
2. led
3. bet
4. wept
5. sank
6. flew
7. spun
8. rang
9. chose
10. froze

PRACTICE 15, p. 7

1. called
2. were watching
3. was humming
4. met
5. saw
6. was cleaning
7. was driving … got
8. was blowing … were bending
9. were playing … was pulling

PRACTICE 16, p. 8

1. 2, 1
2. 2, 1
3. 1, 2
4. 2, 1
5. 1, 2
6. 2, 1
7. 1, 2
8. 2, 1

PRACTICE 17, p. 8

1. had
2. were having
3. stopped … fell … spilled
4. served … came
5. looked … was sleeping … was dreaming … was smiling
6. was working … exploded
7. caused … dropped

PRACTICE 18, p. 9

1. c
2. e
3. b
4. a
5. d
6. g
7. f
8. h

PRACTICE 19, p. 9

1. a
2. a, b
3. a

PRACTICE 20, p. 10

1. 2   take … rains
2. 4   was riding … heard
3. 1   am riding … is repairing
4. 3   rode … forgot
5. 4   was having … crashed
6. 3   had … didn't eat
7. 1   is having
8. 2   has
9. 2   celebrate … are
10. 4   were working … called
11. 3   celebrated … was

PRACTICE 21, p. 10

Across
2. listening
5. think
7. heard
8. thinking

Down
1. went
3. studying
4. ate
6. having
7. have

PRACTICE 22, p. 11

1. is
2. form
3. gather
4. rotate
5. is
6. lasts
7. moves
8. grow
9. damage
10. destroy
11. formed
12. moved
13. cost
14. caused
15. was
16. approached
17. tried
18. was
19. are studying
20. are learning
21. are discovering

PRACTICE 23, p. 12

1. Carole **visits** India every year.
2. In the past, no one **cared** about air pollution.
3. Today we **know** that air pollution is a serious health and environmental problem.
4. I **moved** to Houston two years ago.
5. I was eating dinner when you **called**.
6. The students **are** taking a test right now.
7. Judy **fell** on the slippery floor.
8. I was going **to be transferred** to another university, but I decided to stay here.

CHAPTER 2: PERFECT AND PERFECT PROGRESSIVE TENSES

PRACTICE 1, p. 13

Part I.
1. don't own, need, submit, use, is, use
2. have become, have praised, have expressed
3. has been expanding
4. began
5. had expanded

Part II.
1. T
2. F
3. T
4. T

PRACTICE 2, p. 14
1. shut, shut
2. brought, brought
3. hear, heard
4. lose, lost
5. taught, taught
6. begin, began
7. sang, sung
8. eat, eaten
9. saw, seen
10. throw, thrown
11. became, become
12. went, gone

PRACTICE 3, p. 14
1. a. for
   b. for
   c. since
   d. since
   e. for
   f. since
   g. since
2. a. since
   b. for
   c. since
   d. for
   e. since
   f. since
   g. for

PRACTICE 4, p. 15
1. three weeks ... April 1st ... three weeks
2. two months ago ... January 1st ... two months
3. two weeks ... February 14th
4. six years ... six years ... January, 2016

PRACTICE 5, p. 15
Answers will vary.
1. a. We have known Mrs. Jones for one month.
   b. We have known Mrs. Jones since last month.
2. a. They have lived there for (____) years.
   b. They have lived there since 2014.
3. a. I have liked foreign films since (____).
   b. I have liked foreign films for five years.
4. a. Jack has worked for a software company for one year.
   b. Jack has worked for a software company since last year.

PRACTICE 6, p. 16
1. eaten
2. visited
3. worked
4. liked
5. known
6. worn
7. taken
8. gone
9. ridden
10. been

PRACTICE 7, p. 16
1. have already eaten
2. have won
3. have not written
4. has improved
5. has not started
6. have already swept
7. have you known
8. have made
9. have never ridden
10. Have you ever swum

PRACTICE 8, p. 17
1. a
2. b
3. a
4. b
5. b
6. a
7. a
8. b
9. a
10. b
11. a
12. a

PRACTICE 9, p. 17
1. is
2. has
3. is
4. is
5. has
6. is
7. has
8. is
9. has

PRACTICE 10, p. 18
1. a. became
   b. has been
2. a. has been
   b. has rained
3. a. lived
   b. have lived
4. a. worked
   b. haven't worked

PRACTICE 11, p. 18
1. knew ... have known
2. agreed ... have agreed
3. took ... has taken
4. has played ... played
5. called ... has called
6. sent ... have sent
7. has flown ... flew
8. overslept ... has overslept

PRACTICE 12, p. 19
1. have been talking
2. have spoken
3. has won
4. have you been sitting
5. have sat

PRACTICE 13, p. 19
1. have been playing
2. has played
3. has raised
4. has been lecturing
5. has never missed
6. has slept
7. have been flying
8. has been sleeping
9. have been searching

PRACTICE 14, p. 20
Sample answers
1. In 1999, Janet moved to Canada.
2. In 2000, Janet joined Lingua Schools as a teaching assistant.
3. Janet has been a teacher since 2001.
4. Janet has been teaching / has taught her own class since 2001.
5. Janet has been working / has worked at Lingua Schools since 2000.

PRACTICE 15, p. 20
1. have had ... had been thinking ... been worried ... 've had ... has been ... taken
2. had warned ... has given ... has been crashing ... 've taken

PRACTICE 16, p. 21

1. We had driven only two miles = 1
   we got a flat tire = 2
2. Alan told me = 2
   he had written a book = 1
3. we arrived at the airport = 2
   the plane had already left = 1
4. the dog had eaten the entire roast = 1
   anyone knew it was gone = 2
5. We didn't stand in line for tickets = 2
   we had already bought them by mail = 1
6. Carl played the guitar so well = 2
   he had studied with a famous guitarist = 1
7. the movie ended = 2
   everyone had fallen asleep = 1
8. the professor had corrected the third paper = 1
   he was exhausted from writing comments on the students' papers = 2
9. I had just placed an order at the store for a new camera = 1
   I found a cheaper one online = 2

PRACTICE 17, p. 21

1. had not gotten
2. had not met
3. had never tried
4. had not eaten
5. had not had

PRACTICE 18, p. 21

1. b
2. a
3. b
4. b
5. a
6. b
7. b

PRACTICE 19, p. 22

1. went ... had never been ... didn't take ... was
2. ate ... had never eaten
3. saw ... did ... Had you ever acted ... started

PRACTICE 20, p. 22

1. have been studying
2. had been studying
3. have been waiting
4. had been waiting
5. had been working
6. has been working

PRACTICE 21, p. 23

1. had been listening ... have been dancing ... singing
2. have been waiting
3. had been waiting
4. has been training
5. had been running
6. had been trying ... has been teaching
7. has been performing

PRACTICE 22, p. 23

1. I've **seen** it ten times.
2. I've **been** reading it ...
3. Our guests **left** ...
4. We **have been** studying ...
5. I've **been** having ...
6. ... **had** eaten.
7. ..., so I **ran** ...
8. She **left** ...
9. ..., I **had** celebrated ...
10. B: ... I **have been** holding for more than half an hour!

CHAPTER 3: FUTURE TIME

PRACTICE 1, p. 24
Part I.

Welcome to your ski vacation at Yellowstone National Park! According to the weather forecast, you will have plenty of fresh snow to enjoy this weekend. Before you begin your ski adventure, you need to be aware of possible dangerous situations.

First, make sure you dress appropriately. Temperatures can rise and fall dramatically. Dressing in layers will help you avoid hypothermia and frostbite. A light inner layer of clothing will keep you comfortable and dry. A middle layer will help your body stay warm, and a waterproof outer layer will protect you against rain or snow.

Second, you may encounter wild animals on the trails, but do not approach or try to feed them. You will scare them, and they may become aggressive. In general, animals won't bother you if you don't bother them.

Finally, study a trail map of the ski area so you don't get lost. Stay safe and enjoy your time here!

Part II.
1. T
2. F
3. F
4. F
5. T

PRACTICE 2, p. 24

1. are going to travel
2. are going to tour
3. are going to visit
4. is going to take
5. is going to study
6. is going to do
7. are going to return

PRACTICE 3, p. 25

1. a. will set
   b. is going to set
2. a. will arrive
   b. is going to arrive
3. a. will rain
   b. is going to rain
4. a. will bloom
   b. are going to bloom
5. a. will end
   b. is going to end
6. a. will ... buy
   b. are ... going to buy
7. a. will ... take
   b. am ... going to take

PRACTICE 4, p. 25

1. are
2. will
3. is
4. aren't
5. isn't
6. is
7. won't
8. will

PRACTICE 5, p. 26

1. willingness
2. prediction
3. prediction
4. prior plan
5. willingness
6. prior plan

PRACTICE 6, p. 26

1. a
2. b
3. b
4. a
5. a
6. b

PRACTICE 7, p. 26

1. I'll call him
2. She's going to be / She'll be
3. I'm going to fly
4. We're going to go to the game
5. I'll open it
6. I'm going to teach

PRACTICE 8, p. 27

1. will
2. are going to
3. will
4. A: Are you going to
   B: are going to
5. am going to
6. will
7. will
8. is going to
9. A: am going to
   B: will
10. B: am going to ... will

PRACTICE 9, p. 28

1. retire
2. rings
3. finish
4. take
5. arrives
6. graduates
7. is
8. hear
9. leave
10. get

PRACTICE 10, p. 28

1. b	3. b	5. a	7. a	9. a
2. a	4. a	6. a	8. b	10. a

PRACTICE 11, p. 28

1. will not return / are not going to return ... get
2. gets ... will be / is going to be
3. is not going to be / won't be ... learns ... comes ... asks
4. returns ... is going to work / will work
5. is going to build / will build ... is going to be / will be ... complete
6. hear ... will let
7. will lend ... finish
8. A: will be / is going to be
   B: will be / am going to be

PRACTICE 12, p. 29

1. 'm seeing / am seeing
2. is having / 's having
3. is opening / 's opening
4. are working / 're working
5. are having / 're having
6. are attending / 're attending

PRACTICE 13, p. 29

1. a, b, c	3. a, b	5. a, b
2. c	4. a, b, c	6. a

PRACTICE 14, p. 30

1. I'm sending
2. NC
3. I'm having
4. A: are you doing
   B: I'm studying
5. NC
6. are they getting
7. NC
8. we're moving
9. Is he teaching
10. A: I'm not sending ... I'm visiting

PRACTICE 15, p. 31

1. will be reading / 'll be reading
2. will be flying / we'll be flying
3. will be sleeping / 'll be sleeping
4. will be snowing / 'll be snowing
5. will be watching / 'll be watching

PRACTICE 16, p. 31

1. heals ... will be playing / 'll be playing
2. go ... will be standing / 'll be standing
3. start ... will be attending / 'll be attending
4. have ... will be shopping / 'll be shopping
5. will be attending / 'll be attending ... return

PRACTICE 17, p. 32

1. will already have risen
2. will have been riding
3. will already have landed
4. will have been listening
5. will have drunk
6. will have been flying
7. will have saved
8. will have taught

PRACTICE 18, p. 32

Note: *be going to* is also possible in place of *will*.

1. gets ... will be shining
2. will brush ... shower ... will make
3. eats ... will get
4. gets ... will have drunk
5. will answer ... will plan
6. will have called
7. will be attending
8. will go ... will have
9. finishes ... will take ... returns
10. will work ... goes
11. leaves ... will have attended
12. gets ... will be playing ... will be watching
13. will have been playing
14. will have ... will talk
15. will watch ... will put
16. goes ... will have had ... will be

PRACTICE 19, p. 34

1. Next month, I'm **traveling** / I'm **going to travel** to Europe with my sister.
2. My sister is going to **attend** an academic conference in Amsterdam.
3. While she is attending the conference, I'll **be** touring the city.
4. After Amsterdam, we are going **to** go to Ibiza.
5. When **I'm** there, I'm going to swim in the Mediterranean.
6. My sister and I are going to visit a few other cities in Spain before **we go** to Lisbon.
7. By the end of our trip, we'll have been **traveling** for two weeks.
8. When I return home, I'll have **visited** three European countries.
9. It's going **to** be an awesome vacation.

CHAPTER 4: REVIEW OF VERB TENSES

PRACTICE 1, p. 35

Central Market <u>is offering</u> two classes this month. If you <u>are</u> curious about Indian Food, then Tandoori Nights <u>is</u> the class for you. This class <u>will meet</u> every Friday night from 6:00–8:00. Instructor Elaine Adams <u>had owned</u> a small café in India for several years before she <u>returned</u> to the United States last year. She <u>is going to focus</u> primarily on chicken and vegetarian dishes from northern India. For Spanish food enthusiasts, we <u>are offering</u> Spanish Style Slow Cooking. This class <u>meets</u> Saturday afternoons 2:00–4:00. Instructor Ruben Reyes <u>has been teaching</u> classes at Central Market for nearly twenty years. He <u>has written</u> three cookbooks on Spanish and Mediterranean cuisine. His newest book <u>explores</u> the art of slow cooking. His class <u>introduces</u> students to several main dishes. If you <u>haven't registered</u>, there <u>is</u> still time, but classes <u>are getting</u> full.

1. are, is, meets, explores, introduces, is
2. are offering, are getting
3. returned
4. will meet, is going to focus
5. has written, haven't registered
6. has been teaching
7. had owned

PRACTICE 2, p. 36

1. eat
2. ate … visited … wrote
3. am talking … am answering
4. was studying
5. have asked
6. have been talking
7. will be
8. will be sitting

PRACTICE 3, p. 36

1. has never flown
2. have been waiting … hasn't arrived
3. are … reach
4. didn't own … had owned
5. are having … has been
6. will have left … get
7. went … got … were dancing … were talking … was standing … had never met … introduced
8. was sitting … heard … got … looked … had just backed

PRACTICE 4, p. 37

1. am taking … leave … 'm going … leave … am going to go … is studying … has lived … knows … has promised … have never been … am looking
2. had been raining … dropped … is going to be … changes … wake … will be snowing

PRACTICE 5, p. 37

1. had been
2. met
3. had missed
4. was
5. got
6. took
7. was
8. had grown
9. was
10. was wearing
11. had changed
12. was still
13. asked
14. had gained
15. had turned
16. looked
17. were

PRACTICE 6, p. 38

1. haven't seen
2. is recuperating / 's recuperating
3. happened
4. broke
5. was playing
6. is / 's
7. doing
8. has
9. will / is going to be … 'll / 's going to be

PRACTICE 7, p. 38

1. used
2. use
3. does it consist
4. do teachers use
5. doesn't give
6. doesn't make
7. knows
8. sounds
9. talked
10. fell
11. agree
12. think
13. am taking / 'm taking
14. always asks
15. has been using
16. didn't realize / hadn't realized

PRACTICE 8, p. 39

1. a. is waiting
   b. has been waiting
   c. will have been waiting
2. a. is standing
   b. has been standing
   c. will have stood / will have been standing
   d. will have been standing

PRACTICE 9, p. 39

1. d
2. c
3. a
4. b
5. c
6. c
7. a
8. c
9. b
10. d
11. a
12. d
13. a
14. b
15. c
16. d
17. b
18. d
19. c

PRACTICE 10, p. 41

1. a
2. a
3. b
4. c
5. a
6. c
7. b
8. b
9. d
10. c
11. a
12. a
13. a
14. c
15. c
16. d
17. b
18. a

CHAPTER 5: SUBJECT-VERB AGREEMENT

PRACTICE 1, p. 43

The key to success **is** a lot of practice and hard work. Malcolm Gladwell, in his book *Outliers,* **explains** the 10,000-hour rule. According to Gladwell, 10,000 hours of practice **is** enough to become an expert in almost any field. That's about three hours every single day for ten straight years. Gladwell **provides** several examples.

The Beatle**s were** one of the most successful musical groups in history. Before the Beatles became famous, the band members played near military bases in Germany for eight hours a day, seven days a week. They did this for a year and a half. They had performed about 1,200 times before they reached commercial success. That **is** more than most bands today perform in their entire career.

Another example **is** Bill Gates. Most people **agree** Gates is a computer genius. When Gates **was** in school in the 1960s, computer programming was not very popular. Most schools didn't have computer classes or clubs, but Gates **was** lucky. He attended a school that had advanced technology. He began programming in the eighth grade. By the time he finished high school, he had already completed several hundred hours of computer programming.

Is there a skill you have practiced for 10,000 hours? What do you think? **Is** 10,000 hours enough to make you an expert?

PRACTICE 2, p. 43

1.	a. floats	verb	singular
	b. Boats	noun	plural
2.	a. lives	verb	singular
	b. friends	noun	plural
3.	a. eats	verb	singular
	b. donuts	noun	plural
4.	a. babies	noun	plural
	b. cries	verb	singular

PRACTICE 3, p. 44

1. teach**es**
2. class**es** ... day**s**
3. us**es** ... song**s** ... game**s**
4. finish**es** ... go**es**
5. exercis**es** ... picks

PRACTICE 4, p. 44

1. is
2. are
3. has
4. barks
5. bark
6. is
7. are
8. is
9. are
10. is

PRACTICE 5, p. 44

1. a. is
   b. is
   c. are
2. a. is
   b. are
   c. is
3. a. is
   b. are

PRACTICE 6, p. 44

1. a unit
2. a unit
3. the individual members
4. a unit
5. the individual members
6. a unit

PRACTICE 7, p. 45

1. a. is
   b. are
2. a. is
   b. are
3. a. is ... is
   b. are
4. a. are
   b. is
5. a. is
   b. are

PRACTICE 8, p. 45

1. has
2. were
3. was
4. was
5. is
6. is
7. has
8. has
9. have

PRACTICE 9, p. 45

1. is
2. are
3. are
4. is
5. weren't
6. was
7. aren't
8. isn't
9. has
10. have

PRACTICE 10, p. 46

1. are
2. is
3. is
4. is
5. is ... is ... is
6. isn't
7. isn't
8. is
9. are
10. is
11. are
12. are
13. are
14. are

PRACTICE 11, p. 46

1. is
2. like ... drive
3. is
4. are ... are
5. are ... contains ... are
6. costs
7. is ... is ... are
8. is ... reminds ... makes

PRACTICE 12, p. 47

1. has
2. takes
3. are ... have
4. was ... were
5. take
6. is
7. are ... is
8. has ... are ... were
9. is
10. is
11. is
12. is ... have
13. is
14. speak
15. use

PRACTICE 13, p. 48

1. vote
2. have participated
3. was
4. knows
5. speak ... understand
6. are
7. do ... broadcast
8. are
9. have been
10. has received ... have gone
11. confirms
12. is ... is
13. are
14. has
15. Aren't
16. is
17. begin *4 states begin with the letter A: Alabama, Arkansas, Alaska, Arizona.
18. consists
19. have
20. is
21. Was

PRACTICE 14, p. 48

1. My mother **wears** glasses.
2. Elephants **are** large animals.
3. Your heart **beats** faster when you exercise.
4. Healthy hearts **need** regular exercise.
5. Every child in the class **knows** the alphabet.
6. Some of the **magazines** at the dentist's office are two **years** old.
7. A number of the students in my class **are** from Mexico.
8. One of my favorite **subjects** in school is algebra.
9. **There are** many different **kinds** of insects in the world.
10. Writing compositions **is** difficult for me.
11. The United States **has** a population of over 300 million.
12. Most of the movie **takes** place in Paris.
13. Most of the people in my factory division **like** and **get** along with one another, but a few of the **workers don't fit** in with the rest of us very well.

CHAPTER 6: NOUNS

PRACTICE 1, p. 50

1. center
2. Residents, vegetables, eggs
3. cardboard, glass, metal, paper, fruit
4. Curitiba's
5. household, bus

PRACTICE 2, p. 50

1. cars
2. women
3. matches
4. mice
5. cities
6. donkeys
7. halves
8. chiefs
9. classes
10. feet
11. heroes
12. pianos
13. videos
14. bases
15. bacteria
16. series

PRACTICE 3, p. 51

1. potatoes
2. monkeys
3. thieves ... steroes
4. children
5. teeth
6. beliefs
7. fish
8. species ... kilos

PRACTICE 4, p. 51

1. car**s** ... feather**s**
2. occupation**s** ... Doctor**s** ... Pilot**s** ... airplane**s** ... Professor**s** ... class**es** ... Farmer**s** ... crop**s**
3. design**s** building**s** ... dig**s** ... object**s**
4. computer**s** ... Computers
5. facto**ries** ... employ**s**
6. Kangaroo**s** ... animal**s** ... continent**s** ... zoo**s**
7. Mosquito**s** / Mosquito**es**
8. tomato**es**

PRACTICE 5, p. 51

1. projects ... project
2. groceries ... grocery
3. tomato ... tomatoes
4. pictures ... picture
5. flower ... flowers
6. drugs ... drug
7. eggs ... egg
8. two lanes ... two-lane
9. five-minute ... five minutes
10. sixty-year-old ... sixty years old
11. truck ... truck
12. computers ... computer
13. peanut ... peanuts

PRACTCE 6, p. 52

1. a
2. c
3. b
4. a
5. b
6. c
7. a
8. b
9. a
10. c

PRACTICE 7, p. 52

1. student handbook
2. birthday party
3. government check
4. airplane seats
5. cotton pajamas
6. hotel rooms
7. ten-month-old baby
8. three-day trip
9. three-room apartment
10. five-page paper
11. opera singer
12. stamp collector

PRACTICE 8, p. 53

1. a. parents'
   b. more than one
   c. parents + house
2. a. parent's
   b. one
   c. parent + concern
3. a. cats'
   b. more than one
   c. cats + eyes
4. a. cat's
   b. one
   c. cat + eyes
5. a. Mary's
   b. brother
   c. Mary + brother
6. a. Mary's
   b. brothers
   c. Mary + brothers
7. a. brothers'
   b. more than one
   c. brothers + team
8. a. brother's
   b. one
   c. brother + team

PRACTICE 9, p. 54

1. one
2. more than one
3. more than one
4. one
5. more than one
6. more than one
7. one
8. one

PRACTICE 10, p. 54

1. a. secretary's
   b. secretaries'
2. a. cats'
   b. cat's
3. a. supervisors'
   b. supervisor's
4. a. babies'
   b. baby's
5. a. child's
   b. children's
6. a. actors'
   b. actor's

PRACTICE 11, p. 55

1. mother's
2. grandmothers'
3. teacher's
4. boss'
5. employee's ... employees'
6. men's ... women's ... children's ... girls' ... boys'

PRACTICE 12, p. 55

1. a
2. a
3. a
4. b
5. b
6. b
7. a

PRACTICE 13, p. 55

Count	Noncount
1. eggs ... bananas	food ... bread ... milk ... coffee
2. letters ... magazines ... catalogs ... bills	mail
3. Euros ... pounds ... dollars	money
4. ring ... earrings	jewelry
5. language	vocabulary ... grammar
6. table ... chairs ... umbrella	furniture

PRACTICE 14, p. 56

1. words
2. some
3. cars
4. much
5. sandwich
6. one
7. some
8. very

PRACTICE 15, p. 56

1. hair ... eyes
2. (no change)
3. (no change)
4. (no change)
5. (no change)
6. classes
7. messages

PRACTICE 16, p. 56

1. courage
2. some
3. shoes
4. garbage
5. glasses ... glass
6. glasses ... glass
7. some ... many
8. much ... some
9. hills ... lovely ... damp
10. good

PRACTICE 17, p. 57

1. a ... b ... f ... g ... i
2. e ... h ... j ... l

PRACTICE 18, p. 57

1. many computers
2. much
3. many children are
4. many teeth
5. many countries
6. much
7. much ... much
8. many
9. is ... much
10. much
11. was ... much
12. much
13. many ... volcanoes are
14. many speeches

PRACTICE 19, p. 58

1. a, b, d
2. a, c
3. b, c
4. a, b, c
5. a, b, c
6. c
7. a, c
8. c, d
9. a, b, c
10. a, b, d

PRACTICE 20, p. 58

1. a
2. b
3. b
4. a
5. b

PRACTICE 21, p. 59

1. b
2. a
3. b
4. a
5. c
6. c
7. b

PRACTICE 22, p. 59

1. a little
2. a few
3. a few
4. a little
5. few
6. a few
7. little
8. a few
9. a little ... a little
10. a little ... a little

PRACTICE 23, p. 60

1. state
2. states
3. puppies
4. puppy
5. children
6. child ... chimpanzees
7. neighbors
8. man
9. goose
10. women

PRACTICE 24, p. 60

1. person
2. **the** rights
3. **the** states
4. **Each** senator
5. (*no change*)
6. small state**s**
7. **the** citizens ... (*no change*)
8. citizen

PRACTICE 25, p. 61

1. of
2. Ø
3. of
4. Ø
5. Ø
6. of
7. Ø
8. Ø
9. Ø ... of ... of
10. Ø ... of
11. of ... Ø

PRACTICE 26, p. 61

1. Last month, my brother and I cleaned out my **grandparents'** attic.
2. We found a lot of old **stuff**.
3. There **were** boxes and boxes of books.
4. We even found a 100-**year**-old copy of *The Adventures of Tom Sawyer*.
5. My brother was looking for old comic books, but he didn't find **many** comics.
6. He found a **few** of my uncle's old toys.
7. It was hard **work**, but we had a lot of fun.
8. My grandmother was happy to have a clean attic, and I was happy to have some of her old dishes and **furniture**.
9. One **person's** junk is another person's treasure.

PRACTICE 27, p. 62

Across
3. All
4. some
6. man
8. Every

Down
1. Two
2. One
3. An
5. mice
6. many
7. men

CHAPTER 7: ARTICLES

PRACTICE 1, p. 63

Worry dolls are tiny colorful dolls. They usually come in a group of six to eight dolls in a small wooden box. These dolls are a folk tradition from Guatemala. The dolls are about one-half inch tall. Guatemalan artisans use a short piece of wire to make a frame with legs, arms, a torso, and a head. The artisans wrap yarn around the frame for the shape, and they use pieces of traditional fabric for the costumes. In the folk tradition, children tell a worry to each doll before they go to bed. Then they put the dolls back in the box and close the lid. When the children wake up in the morning, the worries are gone. The dolls have taken away all of the worries.

PRACTICE 2, p. 63

1. indefinite
2. indefinite
3. indefinite
4. definite
5. indefinite
6. definite

PRACTICE 3, p. 63

1. (*no change*)
2. some ingredients
3. (*no change*)
4. some friends
5. some cake ... some music
6. some pictures

PRACTICE 4, p. 64

1. a
2. some
3. an
4. some
5. a
6. some
7. some
8. a
9. a
10. an
11. some
12. some
13. a
14. some

PRACTICE 5, p. 64

1. Ø ... The
2. a ... the
3. a ... The
4. The ... a
5. The ... a
6. the ... a
7. a ... The

PRACTICE 6, p. 65

1. a. plural, generic
   b. singular, specific
2. a. plural, generic
   b. singular, generic
3. a. singular, generic
   b. singular, specific
4. a. plural, generic
   b. singular, specific

PRACTICE 7, p. 65

1. a. Baseball
   b. uniforms
2. a. A data analyst
   b. Data collection
3. a. The clarinet
   b. The violin
4. a. A pecan
   b. Pecans
5. a. A blog
   b. Bloggers
6. a. A meme
   b. Memes

PRACTICE 8, p. 65

1. a
2. b
3. b
4. a
5. a
6. b

PRACTICE 9, p. 66

1. A: a ... a
   B: a
   A: The
2. the
3. a
4. A: a
   B: the
5. a
6. A: the
   B: a
   A: the
   B: the

PRACTICE 10, p. 66

1. Ø Lightning ... a ... Ø
2. a ... the
3. Ø Circles ... Ø
4. A ... a ... the ... the
5. The ... the ... an
6. the ... a ... the ... a ... The ... Ø
7. a ... The

PRACTICE 11, p. 67

1. b	3. a	5. b
2. b	4. b	6. a

PRACTICE 12, p. 67

1. Ø ... the ... Ø	5. Ø
2. the ... Ø	6. A. the ... B. Ø
3. the	7. Ø ... the
4. Ø ... the ... the ... the	8. Ø ... Ø

PRACTICE 13, p. 68

Louis Braille was born in **Ø** France in 1809. He lost his eyesight due to **an** accident when he was **a** child. When he was 15 years old, he developed **a** writing system for **the** blind. **The** writing system consists of **Ø** raised dots. The number and patterns of **the** dots form characters. **The** system is called "Braille" after **the** inventor. Braille has spread from **Ø** France to many countries around **the** world.

PRACTICE 14, p. 68

1. It's beautiful today. **The** sun is shining and **the** sky is clear.
2. I read **a** good book about globalization.
3. **P**enguins live in Antarctica. **P**olar bears don't live in Antarctica.
4. Which is more important — **love or money**?
5. A: What does this word mean?
   B: Do you have **a** dictionary? Look up **the** word in **the** dictionary.
6. A: Watch out! There's a bee buzzing around!
   B: Where? I don't see it. Ouch! It stung me! I didn't see **the** bee, but I felt it!
7. Kevin is going to **the** grocery store. He's getting some ingredients for a pasta dish.
8. Every summer Yoko's family goes camping in **the** Canadian Rockies, but this summer they're going to **the** beach instead.

CHAPTER 8: PRONOUNS

PRACTICE 1, p. 69

1. people	8. one man
2. selfie sticks	9. Disneyland
3. selfie sticks	10. Disneyland's
4. Amanda Campbell	11. selfie sticks
5. the selfie	12. Museums
6. people's	13. visitors
7. many opponents	

PRACTICE 2, p. 69

1. He → Bob
2. They → Mr. and Mrs. Nobriega
3. her → teacher
4. She → baby
5. It → kind
6. them → hawks
7. him → Mr. Frank
8. They → a dog and a cat

PRACTICE 3, p. 70

1. I
2. me
3. them ... They
4. them
5. my ... yours
6. his ... hers ... their
7. She and I ... Our ... us
8. me ... its ... it
9. they ... They ... their
10. its ... its ... It's

PRACTICE 4, p. 70

1. b	5. a, b
2. a	6. a, b
3. a, b	7. a, b
4. a	

PRACTICE 5, p. 71

1. it ... them	5. his or her / their
2. their	6. their ... her
3. his ... her	7. his or her ... its / their
4. it ... They	

PRACTICE 6, p. 71

1. ourselves	5. myself
2. herself	6. yourselves
3. himself	7. yourself
4. themselves	

PRACTICE 7, p. 72

1. is angry at himself
2. introduce myself
3. help yourself
4. pat yourselves
5. talks to herself
6. fix itself
7. laugh at ourselves
8. feeling sorry for himself

PRACTICE 8, p. 72

1. c	3. a	5. c	7. a
2. b	4. a	6. b	

PRACTICE 9, p. 72

1. a	4. a	7. a	10. c
2. a	5. b	8. b	11. b★
3. a	6. c	9. b	

★Oregon, California, Alaska, Hawaii

PRACTICE 10, p. 73

1. another
2. another
3. another
4. another
5. another
6. another

PRACTICE 11, p. 74

1. d
2. f
3. a
4. e
5. b
6. c

PRACTICE 12, p. 74

Hackers look for weaknesses in a computer system. They use the weaknesses to break into computer systems or computer networks. Some hackers break into computer systems because **they** enjoys the challenge. ~~The~~ **O**thers work for large companies. These companies hire hackers to find weaknesses and point **them** out. Afterwards, the companies fix the weaknesses. **AnOther** hackers have criminal motivations. These hacker**s** create viruses and worms. They steal important information~~s~~, such as ~~the~~ passwords and bank account numbers.

A computer virus is piece of code. Viruses attach themsel**ves** to files and programs. They copy themsel**ves** and spread to each computer~~s~~ they come in contact with. They often spread through email messages or Internet downloads. Some viruses slow down computers. ~~An~~**O**thers completely disable computers.

Worms are similar to viruses, but they do not need to attach to ~~a~~ files or programs. Worms use networks to send copies of **their** code to others computers.

There are **many** ways to protect your devices. To start with, keep your firewall on. A firewall is **a** software program or piece of hardware. It protects your device from hackers. Second, install anti-virus software. This software finds and removes viruses and worms. Next, keep your operating system up to date. Newer operating systems have fixed a lot of security problem**s** from old versions. Finally, don't open ~~an~~ attachments or download anything from **an** unfamiliar person.

CHAPTER 9: MODALS, PART 1

PRACTICE 1, p. 75

Thank you for your interest in State University. You <u>must</u> meet certain entrance requirements before you <u>can</u> apply for admission. Each academic department has different requirements. You <u>should</u> read the specific requirements for your major. All applicants <u>must</u> submit a completed application form, entrance exam results, high school or college transcripts, and an application fee.

You <u>must</u> submit your application electronically. All students <u>must</u> take at least one entrance exam. Some majors <u>may</u> require more than one exam. The testing agency <u>will</u> send all entrance exam results directly to the university. Your high school or college <u>may</u> send your transcripts electronically or by mail in a sealed envelope. You <u>may</u> pay the application fee online with a credit card payment or mail a check or money order to the Office of Admissions.

PRACTICE 2, p. 75

1. b
2. a
3. b
4. a
5. c

PRACTICE 3, p. 75

1. a. don't have to
   b. must not
2. a. must not
   b. don't have to
3. a. must not
   b. don't have to
4. a. must not
   b. don't have to

PRACTICE 4, p. 76

1. necessity
2. prohibition
3. lack of necessity
4. necessity
5. lack of necessity
6. necessity
7. necessity
8. necessity
9. prohibition
10. lack of necessity

PRACTICE 5, p. 77

1. a
2. b
3. a
4. c
5. a
6. a
7. c
8. a
9. c
10. b

PRACTICE 6, p. 77

1. b
2. a
3. a
4. b
5. b
6. a
7. a
8. b

PRACTICE 7, p. 78

1. b
2. a
3. b, c
4. a
5. b
6. a

PRACTICE 8, p. 78

1. e
2. g
3. c
4. h
5. b
6. f
7. d
8. a

PRACTICE 9, p. 79

1. is supposed to arrive
2. am supposed to go
3. is supposed to be
4. was supposed to arrive
5. were supposed to come over
6. is supposed to run

PRACTICE 10, p. 79

1. It should be a good movie.
2. It should be available online now.
3. It should be funny.
4. He should appear in a new movie soon.

PRACTICE 11, p. 79

Part I.
1. Kevin is able to speak four languages.
2. Speak up! I am not able to hear you.
3. Are you able to arrive early tomorrow?
4. I am able to understand your point of view.

Part II.
1. Ikuko knows how to create a PowerPoint presentation.
2. Lucy doesn't know how to parallel park.
3. Mazzen knows how to code in JavaScript.
4. Do you know how to fix my computer?

PRACTICE 12, p. 80
1. may / might
2. may / might
3. can / may / might
4. may / might
5. can / may / might

PRACTICE 13, p. 80
1. could you help me
2. Can I help you
3. Would you please give me
4. May I borrow
5. Can you hurry
6. Could you please repeat

PRACTICE 14, p. 81
1. a. cooking
   b. if I cooked
2. a. taking
   b. if I took
3. a. if I opened
   b. opening
4. a. joining
   b. if we joined
5. a. writing
   b. if I wrote

PRACTICE 15, p. 81
1. closing
2. if I closed
3. taking
4. if I went
5. leaving / if we left
6. cooking
7. making / if I made
8. finishing
9. if I used
10. recommending

PRACTICE 16, p. 82
1. a, d
2. b
3. b
4. a, b
5. c
6. b

PRACTICE 17, p. 82
1. Our teacher **can speak** five languages.
2. Oh, this table is heavy! Jim, **can / could / would** you help me move it?
3. We come to class on weekdays. We **don't** have to come to class on weekends.
4. Park here. It's free. You **don't have to** pay anything.
5. When you speak in front of the judge, you **must tell** the truth. You must not tell lies.
6. Pat looks tired. She should **get** some rest.
7. I **am** not able to go to the party this weekend.
8. The children are **supposed** to be in bed by nine o'clock.
9. The Garcias **are** supposed to be here at 7:00, but I think they will be late, as usual.
10. We're going to make chicken for dinner. Why **don't you** join us?
11. Here's my advice about your diet, Mr. Jackson. You **should** not eat a lot of sugar and salt.
12. A: This is wonderful music. **Shall / Why don't** we dance?
    B: No, let's **not** dance. Let's just sit here and talk.

CHAPTER 10: MODALS, PART 2

PRACTICE 1, p. 83

Last Friday's soccer match <u>should have been</u> an easy game for the Wildcats. Their team had an undefeated record this season. However, fans <u>couldn't believe</u> it when the Falcons defeated the Wildcats 5-2. It was the first win of the season for the Falcons. The Falcons <u>must have practiced</u> very hard to achieve their surprise victory. The next Falcons game is this Friday at 6:00 P.M. on their home field. It <u>should be</u> an exciting game!

PRACTICE 2, p. 83
1. would fall … would throw
2. would always say … would come
3. would always bring
4. used to live … would always wipe
5. used to have … would stay … would sleep
6. would tell … would listen

PRACTICE 3, p. 84
1. You had to use blue ink on the form.
2. The students had to memorize 100 new words a week.
3. Sylvia had to cancel her summer vacation plans.
4. Who did you have to call?
5. The children had to get vaccinations.
6. The passengers had to fasten their seat belts because of the turbulent weather.

PRACTICE 4, p. 84
1. should have taken
2. should have turned
3. shouldn't have watched
4. should have visited
5. should have bought
6. should have ordered
7. shouldn't have come … should have stayed
8. shouldn't have changed … should have kept

PRACTICE 5, p. 85
1. should travel
2. should have gone
3. should paint ... should be
4. shouldn't have painted
5. shouldn't have eaten
6. shouldn't drink ... should drink
7. shouldn't have killed
8. should make

PRACTICE 6, p. 85
1. was supposed to arrive
2. were supposed to come over
3. was supposed to give
4. was supposed to snow
5. Were you supposed to turn in

PRACTICE 7, p. 86
1. can't
2. can't
3. can
4. couldn't
5. can't
6. could ... can't
7. couldn't ... Can

PRACTICE 8, p. 86
1. about 50% or less
2. about 95%
3. 100%
4. about 95%
5. about 50% or less
6. 100%
7. about 95%
8. about 50% or less
9. about 50% or less
10. about 50% or less

PRACTICE 9, p. 87
1. a
2. b
3. b
4. a
5. b
6. a
7. b
8. b
9. b
10. a
11. b
12. b

PRACTICE 10, p. 88
1. f
2. a
3. c
4. d
5. b
6. e

PRACTICE 11, p. 88
1. b
2. a
3. b
4. a
5. a
6. b

PRACTICE 12, p. 89
1. must not have remembered
2. couldn't have been
3. may / might not have left
4. must not have heard
5. may / might not have had
6. couldn't have happened

PRACTICE 13, p. 89
1. must have driven
2. must have been / must be
3. must not have known
4. must be
5. must have left
6. must have gone
7. must need
8. must have hurt

PRACTICE 14, p. 90
1. a
2. a
3. b
4. a
5. b
6. a

PRACTICE 15, p. 91
1. e
2. j
3. a
4. f
5. b
6. d
7. i
8. c
9. h
10. g

PRACTICE 16, p. 91
1. will
2. should
3. will
4. should
5. will
6. should
7. must
8. should

PRACTICE 17, p. 92
Modals may vary.
1. could be working
2. should be flying
3. might be sleeping
4. must be kidding
5. must have been kidding
6. might be hiking
7. may not be dating

PRACTICE 18, p. 92
1. have to get
2. should be able to complete
3. won't have to stand
4. will you be able to leave
5. am not going to be able to graduate
6. must not have been able to get

PRACTICE 19, p. 93
1. would rather not say
2. would rather have gone
3. would rather have studied
4. would rather not eat
5. would rather have
6. would rather be sailing

PRACTICE 20, p. 93
1. c
2. c
3. b
4. b
5. c
6. c
7. b
8. c
9. b
10. b

PRACTICE 21, p. 94
Answers may vary.
1. a. It should arrive soon.
   b. It may / might / could have taken off late.
   c. We should have called the airport.
2. a. It may be for me.
   b. It's for me.
   c. It can't be for me.
3. a. He should have responded.
   b. He may not have gotten it.
   c. He must not have gotten it.
   d. He couldn't have gotten it.

4. a. The dishwasher may / might / could be leaking.
   b. It can't be the dishwasher.
   c. A pipe must be broken.
   d. You should call a plumber.
   e. You don't have to call a plumber.

PRACTICE 22, p. 95

Distracted drivers often cause major traffic accidents. In the past, before the widespread use of smartphones, drivers **would / could** be distracted by eating, reading maps, or grooming. These activities **can / might** still cause problems, but one of the biggest issues today is cell phone use. People **can / might** use their phones to talk, text, engage in social media, play games, use navigation systems, check their bank accounts, write shopping lists, listen to music, or look up information on the Internet.

Joy has become a leading advocate against distracted driving since she had an accident last year. She hit another car and blacked out. She **can't / couldn't** remember anything about the accident. According to her phone records, she **must have been** talking on the phone when the accident occurred. Luckily, no one was injured. It **could have been** much worse. She still feels terrible about the accident. She **shouldn't have been using / shouldn't have used** her phone while she was driving.

Advocates like Joy are calling for stricter distracted-driving laws. Several places have already adopted laws against texting or using a cell phone at all while driving. With more distracted-driving laws, the roads **should / can / may** become much safer.

CHAPTER 11: THE PASSIVE

PRACTICE 1, p. 96

The National Weather Service has issued a winter storm warning. Heavy snowfall <u>is expected</u> early this evening. More than a foot of snow accumulation <u>is anticipated</u> by tomorrow morning. Because student safety is our top priority, classes <u>have been canceled</u> for the remainder of the day. The university's business offices <u>are also closed</u>. Residence and dining halls will remain open. Tonight's basketball game <u>has been postponed</u> to next Tuesday. Classes <u>will be canceled</u> all day tomorrow. The university is monitoring the weather closely and will notify the campus community with any additional updates. More details <u>can be found</u> on our school website.

PRACTICE 2, p. 96

1. are	10. has been
2. is being	11. was
3. has been	12. are being
4. was	13. will be
5. was being	14. had been
6. had been	15. will have been
7. will be	16. are
8. is going to be	17. is going to be
9. will have been	18. were being

PRACTICE 3, p. 97

1.	a. A	Henry	visited
	b. P	The park	was visited
2.	a. A	Olga	was reading
	b. A	Philippe	has read
	c. P	Bambi	has been read
3.	a. A	Whales	swim
	b. P	Whales	were hunted
4.	a. P	The answer	won't be known
	b. A	I	know
5.	a. P	Two new houses	were built
	b. A	A famous architect	designed
6.	a. P	The Internet	was invented
	b. A	The Internet	has expanded
7.	P	The World Cup	is seen
	b. A	Soccer fans	watch

PRACTICE 4, p. 98

1. is written		7. will be written
2. is being written		8. is going to be written
3. has been written		9. will have been written
4. was written		10. Was … written
5. was being written		11. Will … be written
6. had been written		12. Has … been written

PRACTICE 5, p. 98

Part I.
1. was painted by Picasso
2. are flown by experienced pilots
3. is going to be sung by a famous singer
4. has been accepted by Yale University
5. will be examined by the doctor
6. is being questioned by the defense attorney
7. was bitten by a dog
8. was being fed by the mother bird
9. won't be persuaded by his words
10. wasn't painted by me … painted by Laura
11. owned by Mrs. Crane… isn't owned by her father anymore
12. weren't signed by me … was signed by someone else

Part II.
13. is going to clean my teeth
14. Did … send that email
15. don't celebrate the Fourth of July
16. Has … sold your house yet
17. haven't caught the thief
18. are cleaning the carpets

PRACTICE 6, p. 99
Checked sentences: 2, 3, 6, 7, 8, 10

PRACTICE 7, p. 100

1. b		7. c
2. b		8. b
3. c		9. a
4. a		10. c
5. b		11. b
6. c		12. a

PRACTICE 8, p. 100

1. b		4. b
2. b		5. a
3. a		

PRACTICE 9, p. 101

1. was invented ... told
2. was established ... was given ... still attend
3. is known ... is related ... live ... became ... were killed ... were saved
4. originated ... like ... gives ... was valued ... was used ... were treated ... is believed

PRACTICE 10, p. 101

1. The chefs prepared the food.
2. The food was prepared yesterday.
3. The rain stopped.
4. A rainbow appeared in the sky.
5. The documents were sent to you yesterday.
6. My lawyer sent the documents to me.
7. The winner of the election was announced on TV.
8. I didn't agree with you about this.
9. What happened yesterday?
10. Something wonderful happened to me.
11. The trees died of a disease.
12. The trees were killed by a disease.
13. A disease killed the trees.
14. I was accepted at the University of Chicago.
15. I was recommended for a scholarship.

PRACTICE 11, p. 102

1. can't be
2. should be washed
3. should have been washed
4. to be finished
5. must have been built
6. have to be paid ... must be sent
7. be permitted
8. ought to be painted

PRACTICE 12, p. 102

1. a. should be made
   b. should make
2. a. should have been made
   b. should have made
3. a. couldn't be spoken
   b. couldn't speak
4. a. must be registered
   b. must register
5. a. has to be paid
   b. have to pay
6. a. must have been
   b. may have been

PRACTICE 13, p. 103

1. g
2. e
3. a
4. h
5. b
6. c
7. f
8. d

PRACTICE 14, p. 103

1. is interested in
2. depends on
3. is married to
4. is scared of
5. bores
6. are made of
7. is composed of
8. is located in
9. is equipped with
10. am prepared for

PRACTICE 15, p. 103

1. by
2. for
3. about
4. in
5. to
6. of
7. with
8. with
9. with
10. with
11. of
12. to

PRACTICE 16, p. 104

1. The plane **arrived** very late.
2. Four people **were** injured in the accident.
3. Bella is married **to** José.
4. People are worried **about** global warming.
5. Astronomers are **interested** in several new meteors.
6. We were **surprised** by Harold's announcement.
7. Spanish **is** spoken by people in Mexico.
8. This road is not the right one. We **are** lost.
9. Pat should try that new medicine. He might **be** helped.
10. Lunch is **being** served in the cafeteria right now.
11. Something unusual **happened** yesterday.
12. Will **the refrigerator be fixed** today?

PRACTICE 17, p. 104

1. crowded
2. hungry
3. lost
4. scared
5. dressed
6. hurt
7. invited
8. chilly
9. stopped
10. elected

PRACTICE 18, p. 104

1. a. excited
   b. exciting
2. a. shocking
   b. shocked
3. a. exhausting
   b. exhausted
4. a. boring
   b. bored
5. a. confused
   b. confusing
6. a. interesting
   b. interested
7. a. thrilling
   b. thrilled

PRACTICE 19, p. 105

1. a. fascinating
   b. fascinated
2. a. exhausting
   b. exhausted
3. a. disappointed
   b. disappointing

PRACTICE 20, p. 105

1. a, d
2. a, b
3. b, c
4. b, d
5. b, c

PRACTICE 21, p. 106

1. frustrating
2. grown ... irritating
3. washing
4. writing
5. frozen
6. depressing ... depressed
7. entertaining
8. known ... spilt
9. comforting ... Barking
10. inspiring ... United ... divided

PRACTICE 22, p. 107

are usually considered ... unprotected ... of ... build ... must be kept ... can range ... is regulated ... maintain ... was inspired ... drawn ... is warmed or cooled ... is called ... amazing

APPENDIX: SUPPLEMENTARY GRAMMAR CHARTS

PRACTICE 1, p. 203

         S   V   O
1. Airplanes have wings.

            S   V   O
2. The teacher explained the problem.

        S   V   O
3. Children enjoy games.

       S   V   O
4. Jack wore a blue suit.

           S   V   O   S   V
5. Some animals eat plants. Some animals eat other

   O
animals.

                                 S   V
6. According to an experienced waitress, you can carry

   O
full cups of coffee without spilling them just by never looking at them.

PRACTICE 2, p. 203

            VI
1. Alice arrived at six o'clock.

        VT
2. We drank some tea.

     VI
3. I agree with you.

     VI
4. I waited for Sam at the airport for two hours.

          VI
5. They're staying at a resort hotel in San Antonio, Texas.

             VI
6. Mr. Chan is studying English.

             VI
7. The wind is blowing hard today.

     VI   VT
8. I walked to the theater, but Janice rode her bicycle.

             VI
9. Crocodiles hatch from eggs.

        VI
10. Rivers flow toward the sea.

PRACTICE 3, p. 203

                    ADJ   ADV
1. Jack opened the heavy door slowly.

    ADJ   ADJ
2. Chinese jewelers carved beautiful ornaments from jade.

    ADJ   ADJ   ADV
3. The old man carves wooden figures skillfully.

      ADJ   ADV   ADJ
4. A busy executive usually has short conversations on the telephone.

      ADJ   ADV ADJ
5. The young woman had a very good time at the picnic

    ADV
yesterday.

PRACTICE 4, p. 204

1. quickly
2. quick
3. polite
4. politely
5. regularly
6. regular
7. usual
8. usually
9. well
10. good
11. gentle
12. gently
13. bad
14. badly

PRACTICE 5, p. 204

1. Ana **always takes** a walk in the morning.
2. Tim **is always** a hard worker.
3. Beth **has always worked** hard.
4. Carrie **always works** hard.
5. **Do you always work** hard?
6. Taxis **are usually** available ...
7. Yusef **rarely takes** a taxi ... .
8. I **have often thought** about ... .
9. Yuko **probably needs** some help.
10. **Have you ever attended** the show ... ?
11. Brad **seldom goes** out ... .
12. The students **are hardly ever** late.
13. **Do you usually finish** your ... ?
14. In India, the monsoon season **generally begins** ...
15. ... Mr. Singh's hometown **usually receives** around... .

PRACTICE 6, p. 205

1. Jim came to class without his books.
2. We stayed at home during the storm.
3. Sonya walked across the bridge over the Cedar River.
4. When Alex walked through the door, his little sister ran toward him and put her arms around his neck.
5. The two of us need to talk to Tom too.
6. Animals live in all parts of the world. Animals walk or crawl on land, fly in the air, and swim in the water.
7. Scientists divide living things into two main groups: the animal kingdom and the plant kingdom.
8. Asia extends from the Pacific Ocean in the east to Africa and Europe in the west.

PRACTICE 7, p. 205

     S   V   O   PP
1. Harry put the letter in the mailbox.

       S   V   PP
2. The kids walked to school.

        S   V   O   PP
3. Caroline did her homework at the library.

           S   V   O
4. Chinese printers created the first paper money

     PP
in the world.

         S   V   PP
5. Dark clouds appeared on the horizon.

                    S   V   O   PP   PP
6. <u>Rhonda</u> <u>filled</u> the <u>shelves</u> <u>of the cabinet</u> <u>with boxes</u>
              PP
   <u>of old books</u>.

PRACTICE 8, p. 205
1. honesty, fairness
2. school, class
3. her illness, her husband's death
4. jail, prison
5. ghosts, UFOs
6. my cousin, a friend
7. mathematics, sports
8. you, your children
9. smoking, cigarettes
10. magazines, a newspaper, websites

PRACTICE 9, p. 205
1. of
2. at
3. from
4. in
5. at
6. of
7. to
8. for
9. on
10. from

PRACTICE 10, p. 206
Situation 1:
1. to
2. to
3. of
4. to
5. with
6. to
7. to

Situation 2:
1. with / by
2. with
3. with
4. of
5. of
6. of, by

PRACTICE 11, p. 206
1. c
2. e
3. b
4. f
5. a
6. g
7. d

PRACTICE 12, p. 207
1. to
2. for
3. from
4. on
5. about
6. for
7. about
8. with
9. on
10. with
11. on
12. of

PRACTICE 13, p. 207
1. for
2. for
3. of
4. to ... for
5. with
6. to
7. on
8. for ... to
9. about
10. of
11. of
12. to / with
13. with
14. to

PRACTICE 14, p. 208

	Question word	Auxiliary verb	Subject	Main verb	Rest of question
1a.	Ø	Can	Chris	live	there?
1b.	Where	can	Chris	live	Ø?
1c.	Who	can	Ø	live	there?
2a.	Ø	Is	Ron	living	there?
2b.	Where	is	Ron	living	Ø?
2c.	Who	is	Ø	living	there?
3a.	Ø	Does	Kate	live	there?
3b.	Where	does	Kate	live	Ø?
3c.	Who	Ø	Ø	lives	there?
4a.	Ø	Will	Ann	live	there?
4b.	Where	will	Ann	live	Ø?
4c.	Who	will	Ø	live	there?
5a.	Ø	Did	Jack	live	there?
5b.	Where	did	Jack	live	Ø?
5c.	Who	Ø	Ø	lived	there?
6a.	Ø	Has	Mary	lived	there?
6b.	Where	has	Mary	lived	Ø?
6c.	Who	has	Ø	lived	there?

PRACTICE 15, p. 209
1. When are you going to the zoo?
2. Are you going downtown later today?
3. Do you live in an apartment?
4. Where does Alex live?
5. Who lives in that house?
6. Can you speak French?
7. Who can speak Arabic?
8. When did Ben arrive?
9. Who arrived late?
10. What is Ann opening?
11. What is Ann doing?
12. What did Mary open?
13. Who opened the door?
14. Has the mail arrived?
15. Do you have a bicycle?
16. What does Zach have in his hand?
17. Do you like ice cream?
18. Would you like an ice cream cone?
19. What would Scott like?
20. Who would like a soft drink?

PRACTICE 16, p. 210
1. How do you take your coffee?
2. What kind of dictionary do you have? (have you? / have you got?)
3. What does he do for a living?
4. Who was Margaret talking to? / To whom was Margaret talking?
5. How many people showed up for the meeting?
6. Why could none of the planes take off?
7. What was she thinking about? / About what was she thinking?
8. How fast / How many miles per hour (OR: an hour) were you driving when the police officer stopped you?
9. What kind of food do you like best?
10. Which apartment is yours?
11. What is Oscar like? (also possible: What kind of person / man is Oscar?)
12. What does Oscar look like?
13. Whose dictionary fell to the floor?
14. Why isn't Abby here?

15. When will all of the students in the class be informed of their final grades?
16. How do you feel?
17. Which book did you prefer?
18. What kind of music do you like?
19. How late is the plane expected to be?
20. Why did the driver of the stalled car light a flare?
21. Which pen do you want?
22. What's the weather like in July?
23. How do you like your steak?
24. How did you do on the test?
25. How many seconds are there in a year?

PRACTICE 17, p. 211
1. How much money do you need?
2. Where was Roberto born? / In what country / city was ...? / What country / city was Roberto born in?
3. How often do you go out to eat?
4. Who(m) are you waiting for? (very formal and seldom used: For whom are you waiting?)
5. Who answered the phone?
6. Who(m) did you call?
7. Who called?
8. How much gas / How many gallons of gas did she buy?
9. What does *deceitful* mean?
10. What is an abyss?
11. Which way did he go?
12. Whose books and papers are these?
13. How many children do they have? [British or regional American: How many children have they?]
14. How long has he been here?
15. How far is it / How many miles is it to Madrid?
16. When / At what time can the doctor see me?
17. Who is her roommate?
18. Who are her roommates?
19. How long / How many years have your parents been living there?
20. Whose book is this?
21. Who's coming over for dinner?
22. What color is Caroline's dress?
23. What color are Caroline's eyes?
24. Who can't go ... ?
25. Why can't Andrew go? / How come Andrew can't go?
26. Why didn't you / How come you didn't answer ... ? (formal and rare: Why did you not answer the phone?)
27. What kind of music do you like?
28. What don't you understand?
29. What is Janie doing right now?
30. How do you spell sitting? [you = impersonal pronoun]
31. What does Xavier look like?
32. What is Xavier like?
33. What does Ray do (for a living)?
34. How far / How many miles is Mexico from here?
35. How do you take / like your coffee?
36. Which (city) is farther north, Stockholm or Moscow? / Of Stockholm and Moscow, which (city / one) is farther north?
37. How are you getting along?

PRACTICE 18, p. 212
1. Did you find your keys?
2. Do you want some coffee?
3. Do you need help?

4. Are you leaving already?
5. Do you have any questions?
6. Are you going up?
7. Did you make it on time?

PRACTICE 19, p. 212
1. Haven't you seen ... ? No.
2. Don't you feel ... ? No.
3. Wasn't he ... ? No.
4. Didn't Dana tell ... ? No.
5. Don't Jill and you work ... ? Yes.
6. Isn't that ... ? Yes.
7. Wasn't she ... ? No.
8. Isn't she ... ? Yes.

PRACTICE 20, p. 213
1. don't you
2. have you
3. didn't she
4. aren't there
5. have you
6. don't you (also possible but less common: haven't you)
7. won't you
8. doesn't he
9. shouldn't we
10. can they
11. are they
12. isn't it
13. didn't they
14. aren't I
15. isn't it

PRACTICE 21, p. 213
1. He's
2. Ø
3. He's
4. Ø
5. She'd
6. Ø
7. She'd
8. Ø
9. We'll
10. They're
11. It's
12. It's
13. Ø
14. Ø
15. We're
16. Ø
17. She's
18. She'd
19. She'd ... we'd
20. he'd

PRACTICE 22, p. 214
1. I don't have any problems. I have no problems.
2. There wasn't any food on the shelf. There was no food on the shelf.
3. I didn't receive any letters from home. I received no letters from home.
4. I don't need any help. I need no help.
5. We don't have any time to waste. We have no time to waste.
6. You shouldn't have given the beggar any money. You should have given the beggar no money.
7. I don't trust anyone. I trust no one.
8. I didn't see anyone. I saw no one.
9. There wasn't anyone in his room. There was no one in his room.
10. She can't find anybody who knows about it. She can find nobody who knows about it.

PRACTICE 23, p. 214

1. We have no time to waste. or We don't have any time to waste.
2. I didn't have any problems. or I had no problems.
3. I can't do anything about it. or I can do nothing about it.
4. You can hardly ever understand her when she speaks.
5. I know neither Joy nor her husband. or I don't know either Joy or her husband.
6. Don't ever drink water from … . or Never drink water from … .
7. … I could barely hear the speaker.

PRACTICE 24, p. 214

1. Hardly had I stepped out of bed … .
2. Never will I say that again.
3. Scarcely ever have I enjoyed myself more … .
4. Rarely does she make a mistake.
5. Never will I trust him again because … .
6. Hardly ever is it possible to get … .
7. Seldom do I skip breakfast.
8. Never have I known a more … .

PRACTICE 25, p. 215

Just add -ing	Drop the final -e	Double the final letter
1.	arriving	
2. copying		
3.		cutting
4. enjoying		
5. filling		
6. happening		
7.	hoping	
8.	leaving	
9.	making	
10.		rubbing
11. staying		
12.		stopping
13.	taking	
14.		winning
15. working		

PRACTICE 26, p. 215

Just add -ed	Add -d only	Double the final letter	Change -y to -i
1. bothered			
2.			copied
3. enjoyed			
4.	snored		
5. feared			
6.		occurred	
7.		patted	
8. played			
9. rained			
10.		referred	
11.			replied
12. returned			
13.	scared		
14.			tried
15. walked			

PRACTICE 27, p. 216

1. rains
2. visited
3. will win
4. is watching
5. will be flying
6. was thinking
7. will be working
8. went … were sleeping
9. fell … will help
10. are swimming

PRACTICE 28, p. 216

1. have
2. had
3. has been
4. was
5. will have been
6. have lived
7. had
8. have
9. had
10. had

PRACTICE 29, p. 216

1. have
2. has been
3. will have been
4. had
5. have
6. had
7. have been waiting
8. has
9. had

PRACTICE 30, p. 217

1. eats
2. ate
3. will eat / 'll eat
4. am eating / 'm eating
5. was eating
6. will be eating
7. have already eaten
8. had already eaten
9. will have already eaten
10. has been eating
11. had been eating
12. will have been eating

PRACTICE 31, p. 218

L.VERB	+	ADJ
1. Ø (no linking verb in the sentence)		
2. looked		fresh
3. Ø		
4. Ø		
5. tasted		good
6. grew		quiet
7. Ø		
8. Ø		
9. Ø		
10. smells		delicious
11. Ø		
12. got		sleepy
13. became		rough
14. Ø		
15. Ø		
16. sounded		happy
17. turns		hot
18. Ø		
19. Ø		
20. appears		certain
21. seems		strange

PRACTICE 32, p. 219

1. clean
2. slowly
3. safely
4. anxious
5. complete
6. wildly
7. honest
8. thoughtfully
9. well
10. fair
11. terrible
12. good
13. light
14. confidently
15. famous
16. fine

PRACTICE 33, p. 219

1. raised
2. rises
3. sat
4. set
5. lay
6. lying
7. laid
8. lie

SPECIAL WORKBOOK SECTION: PHRASAL VERBS

PRACTICE 1, p. 223

1. a. after
   b. over
   c. up
   d. into
2. a. out
   b. into
   c. out
   d. out of
3. a. over
   b. through with
   c. out of
   d. back from
   e. off
4. a. off
   b. up
   c. on
   d. back
   e. in

PRACTICE 2, p. 224

1. passed out
2. Pick out
3. takes after
4. think ... over
5. puts up with
6. passed away
7. show up
8. get along with
9. turn in
10. pass out

PRACTICE 3, p. 224

1. our assignment?
2. a lie. / a story.
3. the city. / the banks.
4. your cigarette. / the lights. / the fire.
5. the war? / the crisis?
6. the problem? / the puzzle?
7. the lights? / the music? / the printer?
8. his classmate. / a girl.

9. chocolate. / smoking.
10. a friend. / a classmate.
11. high school. / college.

PRACTICE 4, p. 225

1. into
2. off
3. on
4. back
5. out
6. up
7. into ... out
8. up
9. up
10. on

PRACTICE 5, p. 226

1. away / out
2. up
3. off / out
4. up
5. off
6. up
7. about, on
8. out of
9. off
10. off ... in

PRACTICE 6, p. 226

1. out
2. back
3. by / in
4. on ... off
5. put ... out
6. up
7. up ... away / out
8. out ... back
9. up
10. on

PRACTICE 7, p. 227

1. up
2. over
3. after
4. up
5. out
6. down
7. up
8. out
9. off
10. up
11. out

PRACTICE 8, p. 228

1. back
2. up
3. out
4. over
5. on ... off
6. in ... out
7. on ... off
8. on ... off
9. up with
10. A: about / on
    B: along with
11. A: over ... in
    B: over